Cambridge Elements

Elements in the Philosophy of Mind
edited by
Keith Frankish
The University of Sheffield

BAYESIAN MODELS
OF THE MIND

Michael Rescorla
University of California, Los Angeles

CAMBRIDGE
UNIVERSITY PRESS

Shaftesbury Road, Cambridge CB2 8EA, United Kingdom

One Liberty Plaza, 20th Floor, New York, NY 10006, USA

477 Williamstown Road, Port Melbourne, VIC 3207, Australia

314–321, 3rd Floor, Plot 3, Splendor Forum, Jasola District Centre,
New Delhi – 110025, India

103 Penang Road, #05–06/07, Visioncrest Commercial, Singapore 238467

Cambridge University Press is part of Cambridge University Press & Assessment,
a department of the University of Cambridge.

We share the University's mission to contribute to society through the pursuit of
education, learning and research at the highest international levels of excellence.

www.cambridge.org
Information on this title: www.cambridge.org/9781009517805
DOI: 10.1017/9781108955973

When citing this work, please include a reference to the DOI 10.1017/9781108955973

First published 2024

A catalogue record for this publication is available from the British Library

ISBN 978-1-009-51780-5 Hardback
ISBN 978-1-108-95829-5 Paperback
ISSN 2633-9080 (online)
ISSN 2633-9072 (print)

Bayesian Models of the Mind

Elements in the Philosophy of Mind

DOI: 10.1017/9781108955973
First published online: December 2024

Michael Rescorla
University of California, Los Angeles

Author for correspondence: Michael Rescorla, rescorla@ucla.edu

Abstract: Bayesian decision theory is a mathematical framework that models reasoning and decision-making under uncertain conditions. The Bayesian paradigm originated as a theory of how people should operate, not a theory of how they actually operate. Nevertheless, cognitive scientists increasingly use it to describe the actual workings of the human mind. Over the past few decades, cognitive science has produced impressive Bayesian models of mental activity. The models postulate that certain mental processes conform, or approximately conform, to Bayesian norms. Bayesian models offered within cognitive science have illuminated numerous mental phenomena, such as perception, motor control, and navigation. This Element provides a self-contained introduction to the foundations of Bayesian cognitive science. It then explores what we can learn about the mind from Bayesian models offered by cognitive scientists.

Keywords: Bayesian decision theory, mental representation, Bayesian cognitive science, subjective probability, conditionalization

ISBNs: 9781009517805 (HB), 9781108958295 (PB), 9781108955973 (OC)
ISSNs: 2633-9080 (online), 2633-9072 (print)

Contents

1 Introduction   1

2 The Probability Calculus   2

3 Bayesian Decision Theory   18

4 Bayesian Cognitive Science   27

5 Realism and Instrumentalism   42

6 Mental Representation   52

7 Anti-representationalism   65

8 Conclusion   75

   Appendix: Foundations of Probability Theory   76

   References   88

1 Introduction

Thomas Bayes was an eighteenth-century minister and mathematician who passed his life in relative obscurity. Upon his death in 1761, his friend Richard Price found among his papers a document entitled "An Essay Towards Solving a Problem in the Doctrine of Chances." Price, recognizing the essay's immense significance, saw to its posthumous publication (Bayes, 1763). Bayes's insights gave birth to what is now known as *Bayesian decision theory*: a mathematical framework that models reasoning and decision-making under uncertain conditions. Named after Bayes due to his founding insights, the framework was first systematically articulated by Pierre-Simon Laplace (1814/1902). Despite frequent vicissitudes in development, reception, and application, the framework attracted increasingly many adherents beginning in the early twentieth century and accelerating as the century progressed (McGrayne, 2011). It currently enjoys great popularity, finding widespread use within statistics (Berger, 1985; Gelman et al., 2014), philosophy (Earman, 1992), machine learning (Murphy, 2023), robotics (Thrun, Burgard & Fox, 2005), physics (Trotta, 2008), medical science (Ashby, 2006), and myriad other disciplines.

Bayesian decision theory originated as a theory of how people *should* operate, not a theory of how they *actually* operate. Nevertheless, cognitive scientists increasingly use it to describe the actual workings of the human mind. Over the past few decades, cognitive science has produced impressive Bayesian models of mental activity. The models postulate that certain mental processes conform, or approximately conform, to Bayesian norms. Bayesian models offered within cognitive science have illuminated numerous mental phenomena, such as *perception*, *motor control*, and *navigation*.

This Element has a two-fold purpose. First, it provides a self-contained introduction to the foundations of Bayesian cognitive science. Second, it explores what we can learn about the mind from Bayesian models offered by cognitive scientists.

On the second front, my main concern is how Bayesian cognitive science relates to *mental representation*. Just as the heart serves to pump blood and the stomach serves to digest food, one of the mind's principal functions is to represent the world. For instance, I have various beliefs about Napoleon: that he was born in Corsica, that he was an emperor, and so on. Thus, the mind somehow reaches beyond itself to represent external reality. In that sense, the mind is a *representational organ*. Historically, most philosophers have agreed that the mind's representational capacity is among its key features. However, prominent scientists and philosophers throughout the past century have questioned whether representation deserves any place in the science of the mind. As a result, controversy continues to fester over the explanatory value of mental representation. *Representationalists* such as Burge (2010; 2022), Fodor (1975; 1987; 2008), Peacocke (1994; 1999), Pylyshyn (1984), and Shea (2018) insist that mental representation plays a vital role within the scientific explanation of various core mental phenomena. *Anti-representationalists* as varied as Chemero (2009), Churchland (1981), Field (2001), Quine (1960), Ramsey (2007), Stich (1983), and van Gelder (1992) reject this position.

I will argue that Bayesian cognitive science assigns mental representation a central explanatory role. Bayesian models of perception, motor control, navigation, and other core mental activities posit representational mental states. Explanations supplied by the models characterize both explananda and explanantia in thoroughly representational terms. So Bayesian cognitive science presupposes the traditional picture of the mind as a representational organ. It invests that picture with unprecedented empirical substance through well-confirmed, mathematically rigorous models.

Sections 2 and 3 present key elements of Bayesian decision theory. Section 4 surveys how cognitive scientists use the Bayesian framework to model mental activity. Section 5 articulates a *realist* stance towards Bayesian models of the mind: when a Bayesian model is explanatorily successful, we have good reason to believe that the model describes actual mental states and processes with at least approximate accuracy. Sections 6 and 7 argue that representational properties of mental states figure crucially in explanations provided by Bayesian cognitive science. My conclusion: Bayesian modeling supports a representationalist perspective on the mind.

My exposition contains more mathematics than most writings on philosophy of mind. The technical content reflects my conviction that fully understanding mental representation requires familiarity with the mathematical language used by scientists to study mental representation. I hope that this Element will help some readers achieve the requisite familiarity and will promote greater appreciation for the benefits that such familiarity affords. To keep the text as accessible as possible, I have confined many technical details to the Appendix.

2 The Probability Calculus

The core notion of Bayesian decision theory is *credence*, or *subjective probability*—a quantitative measure of the degree to which an agent believes a hypothesis. I may have low credence that a meteor shower occurred five days ago, higher credence that Seabiscuit will win the race tomorrow, and even higher credence that Napoleon was born in Corsica. An agent's credence in hypothesis H is notated as $P(H)$. Credences are psychological facets of the individual agent, not objective chances or frequencies out in the world. The agent's credences need not track any *objective probabilities* that inhere in mind-independent reality. To illustrate, suppose that a biased coin has objective chance 0.3 of landing heads. I may mistakenly believe that the coin is fair and therefore assign subjective probability 0.5 to the hypothesis that it will land heads. Then my credence departs dramatically from the objective chance of heads.

What is it to attach a credence to a hypothesis? What does it mean for an agent to set $P(H) = x$ as opposed to $P(H) = y \neq x$? Beginning with Ramsey (1931) and de Finetti (1937/1980), many authors have tried to answer these questions (Erikkson & Hájek, 2007). In practice, contemporary Bayesians usually leave the questions unanswered. They take the notion of credence as primitive, without providing noncircular necessary and sufficient conditions for an agent to attach a credence to a hypothesis. This is the strategy pursued within Bayesian cognitive science, and it is the strategy I will pursue.

Bayesian decision theory was given a secure mathematical grounding by Kolmogorov (1933/1956), who articulated axioms for probability in his landmark *Foundations of the Theory of Probability*. The axioms are not specific to subjective probability; they apply equally to objective probability. Section 2 expounds basic aspects of Kolmogorov's axiomatization, which is sometimes called *the probability calculus*. Section 3 discusses how Bayesians use the probability calculus to model uncertainty.[1]

2.1 Sets of Outcomes

Kolmogorov's axiomatization uses *set theory* as a basis for probability theory. The central notion of set theory is *membership*:

$$\omega \in A,$$

meaning that ω *is a member of set A*. We also say that ω *belongs to A*.

In Kolmogorov's axiomatization, probabilities attach to *sets of outcomes* drawn from an *outcome space* Ω. To illustrate, suppose we want to model probabilities over the result of a player rolling a six-sided die. We may take the outcome space to be

$$\Omega = \{1,\ 2,\ 3,\ 4,\ 5,\ 6\},$$

---

[1] Readers seeking a more leisurely introduction to Bayesian decision theory have many options pitched at varying levels of difficulty. Hacking (2001) is aimed at philosophers and makes relatively modest mathematical demands. Stone (2013) occupies an intermediate level of difficulty. Berger (1985) and Gelman et al. (2014) are standard statistical references and are more mathematically demanding.

that is, the set containing elements 1, 2, 3, 4, 5, and 6. The hypothesis *that the player rolls an even number* corresponds to the set

$$\{2, 4, 6\}.$$

Similarly, suppose we seek to define probabilities over possible results of a horse race. We can specify an outcome by describing the order in which the horses finish. Ω contains each such outcome. The hypothesis *that Seabiscuit wins the race* corresponds to the set

$$\{\omega : \text{Seabiscuit finishes before every other horse in } \omega\},$$

that is, the set of outcomes in which Seabiscuit finishes before every other horse.

Philosophers commonly assume that probabilities attach to *propositions*. In the scientific and mathematical literature, one rarely finds any appeal to propositions. Instead, researchers follow Kolmogorov in attaching probabilities to sets. Under certain assumptions, one can recapture talk about "propositions" within Kolmogorov's setting. One can treat Ω as containing *possible worlds*, and one can analyze propositions as *sets of possible worlds* (Stalnaker, 1984). These assumptions are not mandated by Kolmogorov's axiomatization. For example, the simple outcome space $\{1, 2, 3, 4, 5, 6\}$ is allowed by Kolmogorov's axiomatization, even though its elements are not possible worlds.

When probabilities attach to sets of outcomes, elementary set-theoretic operations mimic the propositional operations *negation*, *conjunction*, and *disjunction*:

- **Negation corresponds to complementation**. The *complement* of set A is the set A^c containing all elements that are in Ω but not in A. See Figure 1. The hypothesis *that the player rolls 1* is the set

  $$\{1\},$$

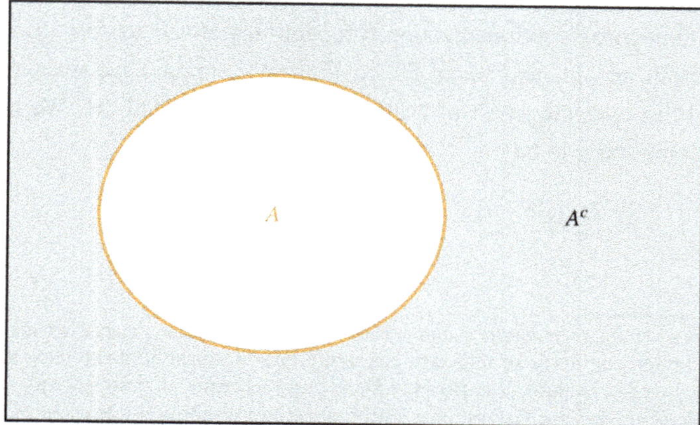

Figure 1 Ω is the rectangle. A is the ellipse. A^c is shaded gray.

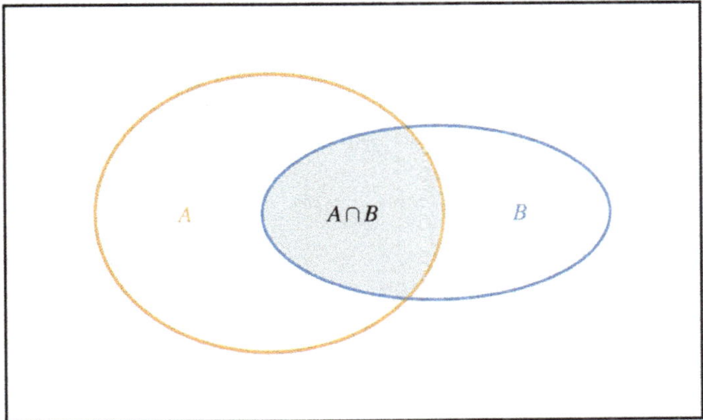

Figure 2 A and B are overlapping sets. Their intersection $A \cap B$ is shaded gray.

while the hypothesis *that the player does not roll 1* is its complement

$$\{1\}^c = \{2, 3, 4, 5, 6\}.$$

- *Conjunction corresponds to intersection.* The *intersection* of A and B is the set containing all elements that are in both A and B. The intersection is written as $A \cap B$. See Figure 2. The hypothesis *that the player rolls an even number and the player rolls a number greater than 3* is the intersection

$$\{2, 4, 6\} \cap \{4, 5, 6\} = \{4, 6\}.$$

If we intersect together disjoint sets (i.e. sets that share no members), then the result is the empty set $\emptyset$ containing no members. The hypothesis *that the player rolls an even number and the player rolls an odd number* is

$$\{2, 4, 6\} \cap \{1, 3, 5\} = \emptyset.$$

- *Disjunction corresponds to union.* The *union* of A and B is the set containing all elements that are in A or B. The union is written as $A \cup B$. See Figure 3. The hypothesis *that the player rolls 1 or the player rolls 4* is the union

$$\{1\} \cup \{4\} = \{1, 4\}.$$

By iteratively applying set-theoretic operations, Kolmogorov replicates the formation of logically complex sentences or propositions.

In simple applications, such as a die roll or horse race, the outcome space Ω is finite. Many applications require Ω to be infinite. For example, consider an asteroid's speed as it enters our solar system. There are infinitely many possible

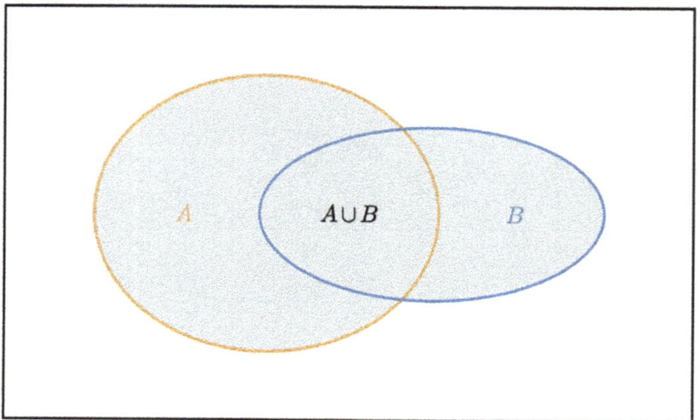

Figure 3 *A* and *B* are overlapping sets. Their union $A \cup B$ is shaded gray.

asteroid speeds. If we want to model probabilities over possible asteroid speeds, we need an infinite outcome space.

2.2 Axioms of the Probability Calculus

In probability theory, sets of outcomes are called *events*. The probability calculus contains three axioms that govern the assignment of probabilities to events:

Axiom 1: Probabilities are real numbers between 0 and 1,

where a *real number* is any number that can be expressed as a decimal. As applied to subjective probability, Axiom 1 sets a scale for degrees of belief. 1 is the maximal possible degree of belief. 0 is the minimum. When an agent assigns probability 1 to an event, we say that the agent is *certain* of the event.

Axiom 2: $P(\Omega) = 1$.

Intuitively: Ω exhausts all relevant possibilities, so it must receive maximal degree of belief.

Axiom 3: Additivity.

To elucidate additivity, suppose that H_1 and H_2 are disjoint events. For example, let H_1 be the hypothesis *that Seabiscuit wins the race* and H_2 the hypothesis *that War Admiral wins the race*. Consider the union $H_1 \cup H_2$: the hypothesis *that Seabiscuit wins the race or War Admiral wins the race*. Additivity requires that:

$$P(H_1 \cup H_2) = P(H_1) + P(H_2).$$

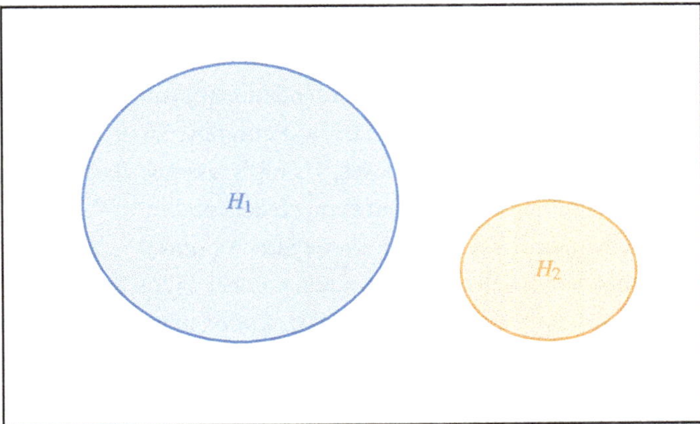

Figure 4 H_1 and H_2 are disjoint events. Additivity requires that their union (the total shaded area) receive a probability equal to the sum of the probabilities assigned to them individually.

In general, the probability that either of two disjoint events occurs is found by adding together the probabilities assigned to the individual events. See Figure 4. As discussed in Section A2, Kolmogorov ultimately uses a somewhat stronger version of additivity than I have articulated here.

Axioms 1–3 can be applied to objective probabilities or to subjective probabilities. Applied to objective probabilities, they are construed as constraints that probabilities *do in fact* satisfy. Applied to subjective probabilities, they are construed as constraints that probabilities *should* satisfy: an agent is rational to the extent that her credences satisfy the axioms.[2]

The core tenet of Bayesian decision theory is that credences should conform to the probability calculus axioms. Since Bayesians advance the probability calculus axioms as normative constraints, we may ask why these particular axioms are supposed to be rationally privileged. Why is someone who conforms

---

[2] An alternative formulation of the probability calculus centers on *sentences* rather than *sets*. Whereas Kolmogorov assigns probabilities to sets of outcomes, the alternative formulation assigns them to *sentences* drawn from a suitable language. One can develop probability theory on this alternative sentential basis (e.g. Gaifman & Snir, 1982). Some Bayesian models found in cognitive science, especially models of high-level cognition, use sentential rather than set-theoretic axiomatization (Piantadosi & Jacobs, 2016). For example, sentential models have been successfully applied to *causality* (Goodman, Ullman, & Tenenbaum, 2011), *kinship* (Katz et al., 2008), and *analogical reasoning* (Cheyette & Piantadosi, 2017). However, set-theoretic axiomatization underlies the vast bulk of research in Bayesian cognitive science, including all or virtually all research into relatively low-level processes such as perception, motor control, and navigation. This Element focuses exclusively on models that use Kolmogorov's set-theoretic axiomatization. Much of what I say about those models would apply, in suitably modified form, to models that use sentential axiomatization.

to the axioms rationally superior to someone who violates them? A large literature, stretching back to Ramsey (1931) and de Finetti (1937/1980), seeks to answer this question by providing a foundational justification for the probability calculus axioms (Easwaran, 2011a; Pettigrew, 2019; Pettigrew, 2020; Weisberg, 2009). For present purposes, I simply assume that the probability calculus axioms are rational constraints on credence.

From a mathematical perspective, we regard Axioms 1–3 as constraints on a function P that maps each event H to a real number $P(H)$. When P satisfies all three constraints, it is called a *probability distribution* or a *probability measure*.[3]

2.3 Random Variables

Probability theory assigns a central role to *random variables*. Intuitively, a random variable uses real numbers to model a specific aspect of a probabilistic situation. To illustrate, suppose that the outcome space Ω contains possible worlds in which an asteroid is hurtling towards Earth. Let X be a function that carries each possible world to the asteroid's speed in that world as the asteroid enters our solar system (where speed is measured using canonical units, such as meters/sec). So

$$X(\omega) = x$$

means that the asteroid has speed x in world ω as it enters our solar system. X is a function from Ω (a set of possible worlds) to $\mathbb{R}$ (the set of real numbers). More generally, suppose we have an outcome space Ω. A *random variable* is a function that carries each outcome ω to a real number x:

$$X(\omega) = x \, .$$

A rigorous definition of "random variable" is given in Section A3, but for present purposes we may operate at a more intuitive level.

We can use a random variable X to define various events of interest. Continuing the asteroid example, take the hypothesis *that the asteroid's speed falls between a and b*. To codify the hypothesis more formally, our first step is to consider the interval $[a, b]$. See Figure 5. Our second step is to collect together all the possible worlds mapped by X into that interval. In other words, we consider the set of possible worlds ω such that $a \leq X(\omega) \leq b$:

$$\{\omega : a \leq X(\omega) \leq b\}.$$

---

[3] These locutions are extensionally equivalent, although they have somewhat different connotations. See Fristedt & Gray (1997, p. 12) for helpful discussion.

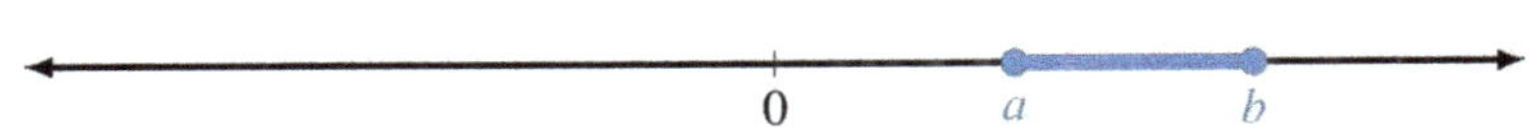

Figure 5 An interval $[a, b]$ lying in $\mathbb{R}$.

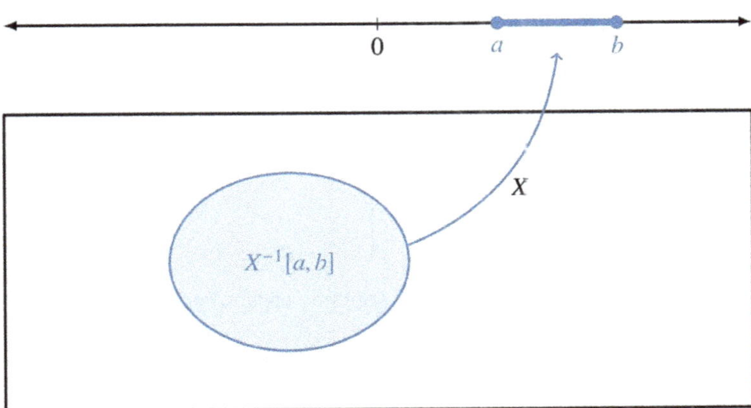

Figure 6 Ω is the rectangle. $X^{-1}[a, b]$ contains the outcomes mapped by X into the interval $[a, b]$.

This set is notated as $X^{-1}[a, b]$. It contains those possible worlds where the asteroid's speed falls between a and b, so it codifies the hypothesis *that the asteroid's speed falls between a and b*. More generally, given a random variable X defined on outcome space Ω, $X^{-1}[a, b]$ codifies the hypothesis *that X's value falls between a and b*. See Figure 6.

As a second illustration, consider the asteroid's position when it hits the earth's surface. We can describe asteroid position using an ordered pair (x, y) drawn from a canonical coordinate system (e.g. longitude and latitude). We now want a function X that maps each possible world ω to an x-coordinate and a second function Y that maps ω to a y-coordinate. The conjunction

$$X(\omega) = x \,\&\, Y(\omega) = y$$

means that the asteroid lands at location (x, y) in possible world ω. Taken together, X and Y map Ω (a set of possible worlds) into $\mathbb{R}^2$ (the set of ordered pairs of real numbers). We may use X and Y to define various events of interest. For example, consider the rectangle depicted in Figure 7. Call this rectangle *REC*. We would like to codify the hypothesis *that the asteroid lands within REC*. To do so, we collect together all the possible worlds where the asteroid

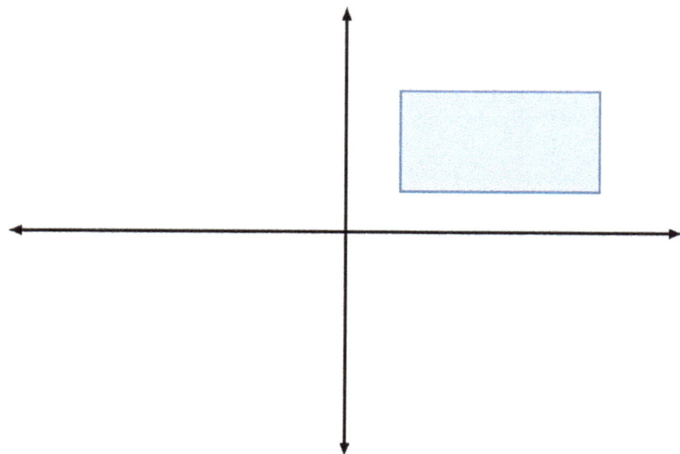

Figure 7 Rectangle *REC* contains ordered pairs (x, y).

lands within *REC*. In other words, we consider the set of possible worlds ω such that $(X(\omega), Y(\omega))$ belongs to *REC*:

$$\{\omega : (X(\omega), Y(\omega)) \in REC\}.$$

This set contains exactly those possible worlds where the asteroid lands within *REC*, so it codifies the hypothesis *that the asteroid lands within REC*. See Figure 8.

Random variables are tremendously useful in probability theory. The underlying outcome space Ω is often hard to describe or otherwise resistant to direct mathematical analysis. In particular, it is not easy to define probabilities directly over sets of possible worlds. A random variable shifts attention from Ω to a friendlier outcome space, such as $\mathbb{R}$ or $\mathbb{R}^2$, greatly augmenting our expressive and analytic power. I will illustrate in the next section.

2.4 Probability Density

Suppose we take $\mathbb{R}$ as the outcome space, so that probabilities attach to sets of real numbers. $\mathbb{R}$ is a natural choice when we are modeling a variable that takes real numbers as values. For example, if X is a random variable that models asteroid speed, then the probability assigned to $[a, b]$ is the probability that the asteroid's speed falls between a and b.

It is often possible to specify a probability distribution over sets of real numbers using a *probability density function*. A probability density function (pdf) is a nonnegative function over $\mathbb{R}$ such that the total area under the curve is 1. Figure 9 illustrates with a sample pdf $p(x)$. When you see an image like

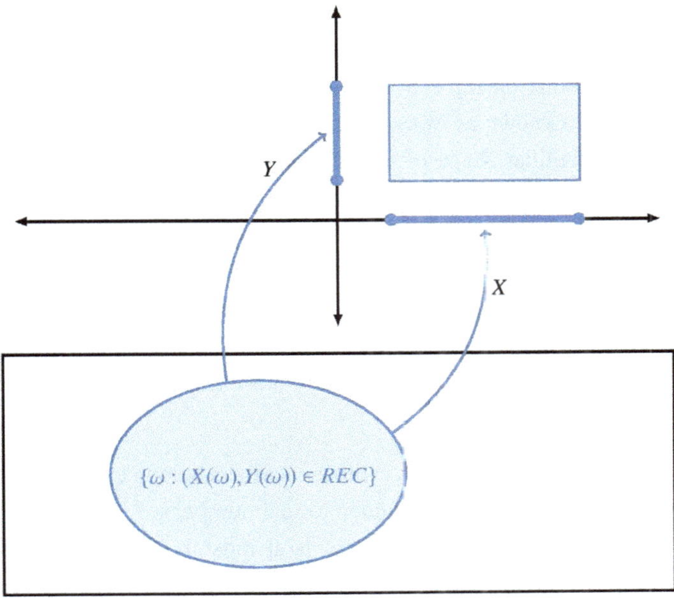

Figure 8 $\{\omega : (X(\omega), Y(\omega)) \in REC\}$ contains the outcomes mapped by X and Y into REC.

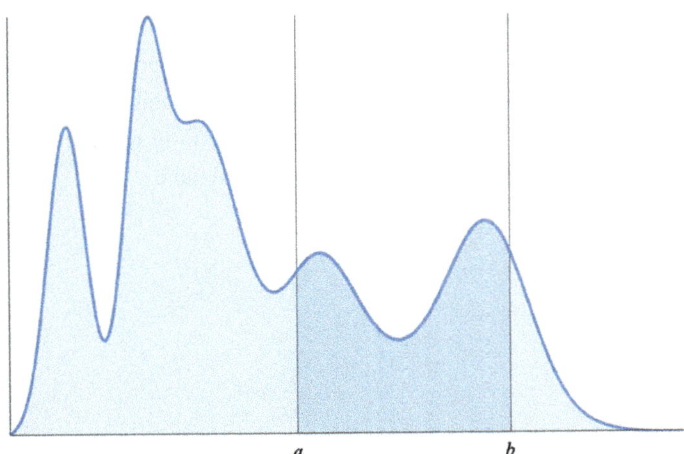

Figure 9 The curve is the pdf. The area under the curve between a and b is the probability assigned to $[a, b]$.

Figure 9, it is vital to remember that the numbers on the vertical axis are *not* probabilities. They are probability *densities*. Probabilities are determined by probability densities as follows: the probability assigned to an interval $[a, b]$ is the area under $p(x)$ stretching from a to b. In this manner, the pdf (a function from *real numbers* to *probability densities*) determines a probability distribution (a function from *sets of real numbers* to *probabilities*).

The most famous example of probability density is the class of *Gaussian distributions*, also known as *Normal distributions*. The pdf for a Gaussian distribution has the familiar shape of a "bell curve." A Gaussian pdf is completely described by two parameters: its *mean* and its *variance* (a measure of how "spread out" the curve is from the mean). See Figures 10 and 11. Many variables encountered in nature are well-described, at least approximately, using a Gaussian pdf.

Bayesian cognitive scientists tend to be cavalier about the distinction between *probability* and *probability density*. My own previous writings have also treated the distinction quite sloppily. Nevertheless, the distinction is an important one:

- Probabilities are assigned to sets whose members belong to an outcome space Ω. Probability densities are assigned to real numbers.
- The probability assigned to an event is at most 1. In contrast, probability density may be much greater than 1. A pdf can attain very high values, so long as total area under the curve is 1.

As is customary in the literature, I notate probability using an upper case P and probability density using a lower case p.

To see the distinction between probability and probability density in action, consider a probability distribution P with a Gaussian pdf $p(x)$. $p(x)$ assigns densities to *individual real numbers*. P assigns probabilities to *sets of real numbers*: the probability assigned to interval $[a, b]$ is the area under $p(x)$ stretching from a to b. For every real number s, we have

$$p(s) > 0.$$

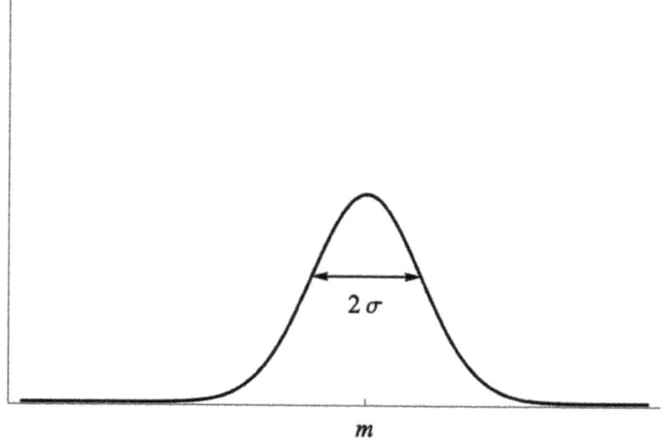

Figure 10 A Gaussian pdf with mean m and variance σ^2.

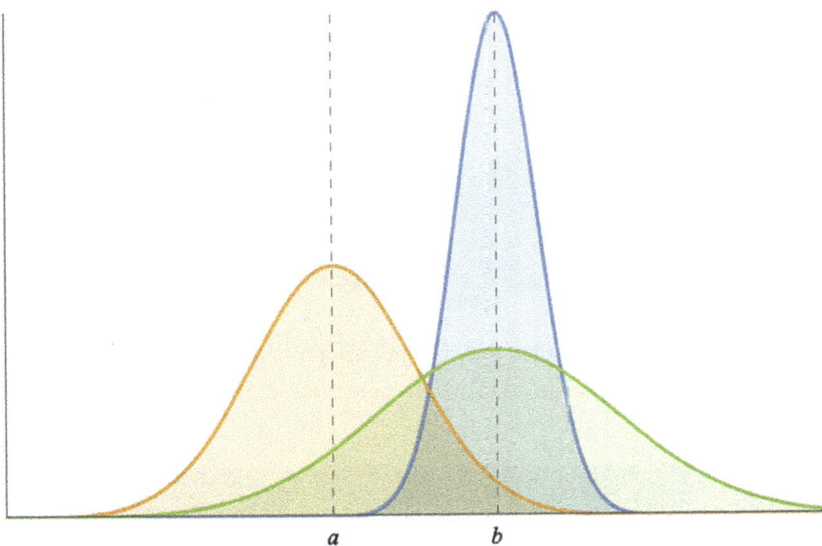

Figure 11 Three Gaussian pdfs. The orange pdf has mean a. The blue and green pdfs have mean b. The blue pdf has smaller variance than the green pdf. The orange pdf has intermediate variance.

What about the probability assigned to $\{s\}$, that is, the set whose sole member is s? It is not hard to show that

$$P(\{s\}) = 0.$$

Intuitively: the probability assigned to $\{s\}$ is the area under $p(x)$ stretching from s to s, and that area is simply 0. Thus, the *probability density $p(s)$* assigned to an individual point s differs from the *probability $P(\{s\})$* assigned to the event $\{s\}$. Note that, even though each individual event $\{s\}$ receives probability 0, we nevertheless have

$$P([a, b]) > 0$$

when $a \neq b$. This may at first seem surprising, but it does not violate the probability calculus axioms. The axioms allow each event $\{s\}$ to receive probability 0 even while $[a, b]$ receives positive probability.

The notion of pdf generalizes to $\mathbb{R}^2$. In the two-dimensional case, a probability distribution assigns probabilities to sets containing ordered pairs (x, y). For example, suppose we are modeling the asteroid's position (x, y) when it hits the earth's surface. The probability distribution assigns a probability to each rectangle: this is the probability that the asteroid's position falls within that rectangle. In the two-dimensional case, a pdf is a nonnegative function $p(x, y)$

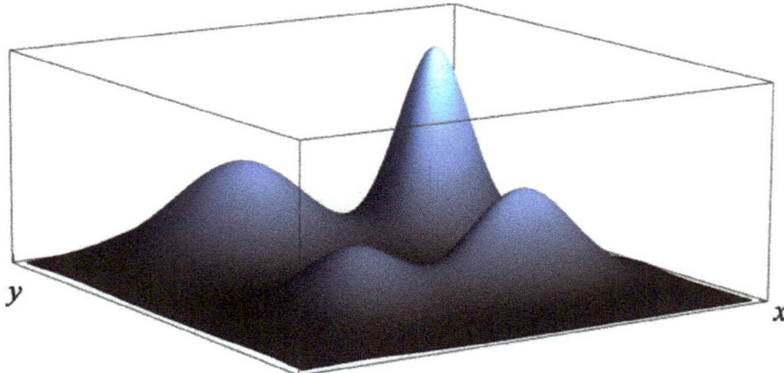

Figure 12 A two-dimensional pdf. The pdf assigns a nonnegative value to each ordered pair (x, y). Total volume under the curve is 1.

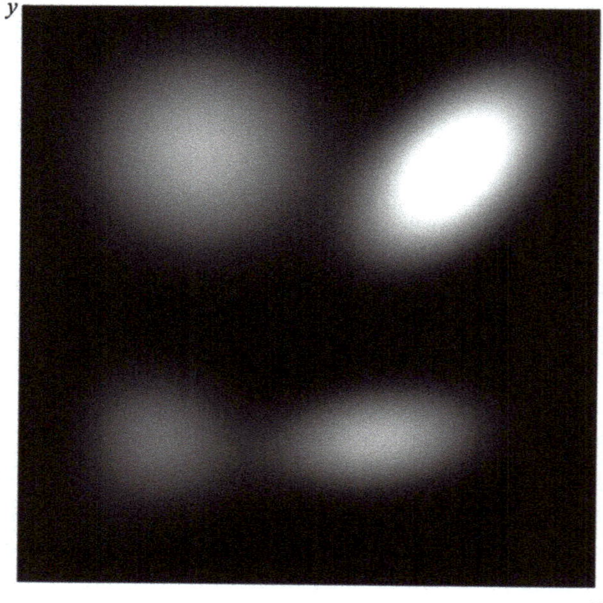

Figure 13 An alternative depiction of the pdf from Figure 12. Lighter shading signifies higher probability density assigned to point (x, y).

over $\mathbb{R}^2$ such that the total volume under the curve is 1. The probability assigned to a region is the volume under the curve in that region. See Figures 12, 13, and 14. A famous example is the class of *two-dimensional Gaussian distributions*, which generalize one-dimensional Gaussians to $\mathbb{R}^2$. See Figures 15 and 16. Once again, it is crucial to distinguish between *probability* and *probability density*. Probability densities attach to ordered pairs (x, y). Probabilities attach to *sets* of ordered pairs.

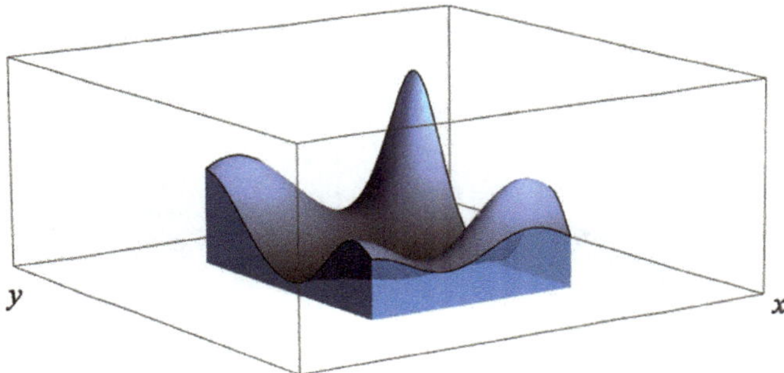

Figure 14 The pdf from Figure 12, restricted to the portion lying over
a rectangle in the (x, y) plane. The volume under this portion of the pdf is the
probability assigned to the rectangle.

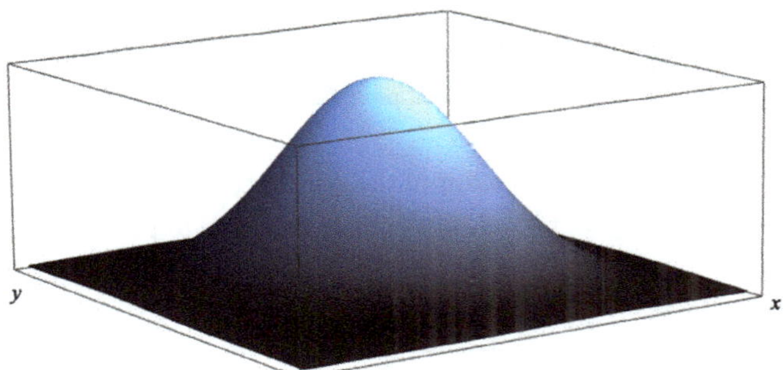

Figure 15 A two-dimensional Gaussian pdf.

2.5 Conditional Probability

Conditional probabilities are fundamental to probability theory. Intuitively, the
conditional probability $P(A|B)$ is the probability of *A given B*. For example, we
can consider the probability that Seabiscuit wins the race *given that he is sick*. In
elementary applications, conditional probability is defined through the *ratio
formula*:

$$P(A|B) =_{df} \frac{P(A \cap B)}{P(B)}.$$

See Figure 17. As Figure 17 illustrates, the unconditional probability of A may
differ significantly from the probability of A given B.

The ratio formula is only well-defined when $P(B) > 0$. Yet scientific practice
frequently requires conditional probabilities when $P(B) = 0$. For example, we
might want conditional probabilities regarding how long an asteroid will take to

Figure 16 An alternative depiction of the pdf from Figure 15. Lighter shading signifies higher probability density assigned to point (x, y).

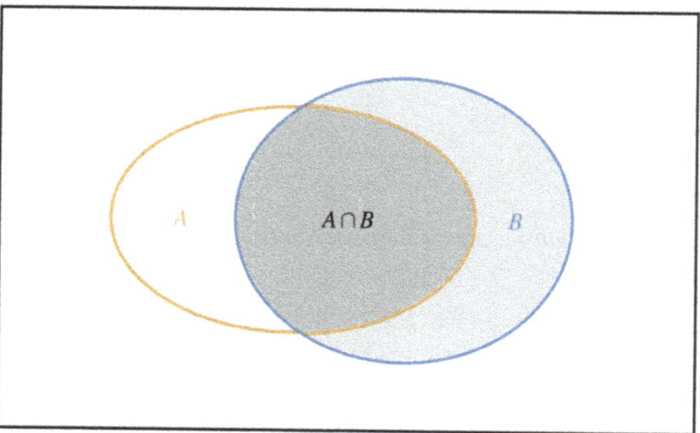

Figure 17 To compute $P(A|B)$ using the ratio formula, divide $P(A \cap B)$ by $P(B)$. For heuristic purposes, assume that the probability assigned to a region is proportional to the region's area. Then Figure 17 depicts a case where $P(A)$ is much smaller than $P(A|B)$.

reach Earth *given that the asteroid has speed s when it enters the solar system.*
Suppose that our probability distribution P over asteroid speed has a pdf $p(x)$.
As indicated in Section 2.4, the probability assigned to the event $\{s\}$ is 0:

$$P(\{s\}) = 0.$$

Thus, we cannot use the ratio formula to define probabilities conditional on $\{s\}$. As this example illustrates, an adequate treatment must move beyond the ratio formula, delineating conditional probabilities $P(A|B)$ for cases where $P(B) = 0$.

When P is given by a two-dimensional pdf, a fairly straightforward notion of conditional probability is available. Consider a two-dimensional pdf $p(x,y)$, such as in Figure 12 or Figure 15. We can use $p(x,y)$ to define a *conditional* density $p(y|x)$. Intuitively, $p(y|x)$ is a density over *y conditional on X having value x.* For each possible value x of the random variable X, the conditional pdf yields a *one-dimensional* pdf over y alone. Basically, $p(y|x)$ is defined by holding x fixed in $p(x,y)$ while allowing y to vary. The only hitch is that the area under the resulting curve may not be 1, while the definition of pdf requires the area under the curve to be 1. Hence, one must also divide by a *normalization constant* to ensure that probabilities sum to 1. Figures 18 and 19 illustrate using the pdf from Figure 12. To compute $p(y|a)$, we hold X fixed at value a while allowing y to vary. The result is the cross-section curve depicted in Figure 18. To convert the cross-section curve into a pdf over y, we must divide by a normalization constant to ensure that area under the curve is 1. The normalized curve is depicted in Figure 19. Figures 18 and 19 also depict the same procedure

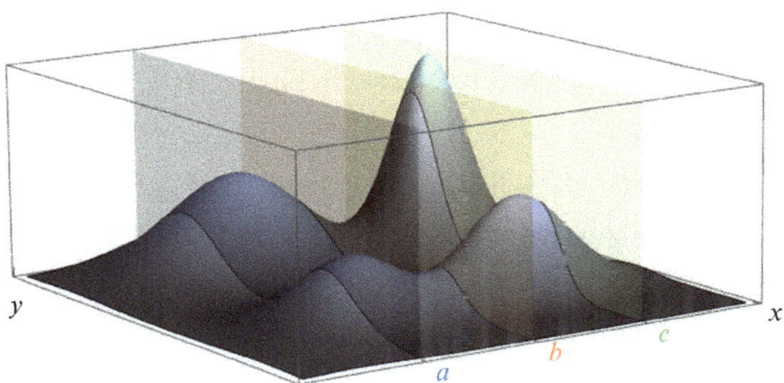

Figure 18 Conditional densities for the pdf from Figure 12. To compute $p(y|a)$, we fix X's value at a and consider the resulting cross-section curve. Area under the cross-section curve may not be 1. Thus, we divide by a *normalization constant* to ensure that area under curve is 1. The result of dividing by the normalization constant is depicted in Figure 19. Similarly for $p(y|b)$ and $p(y|c)$.

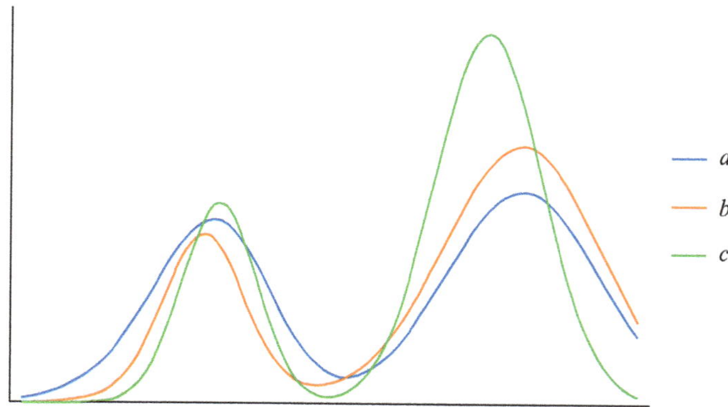

Figure 19 Three one-dimensional pdfs over *Y* induced by Figure 18. The blue pdf is $p(y|a)$, the orange pdf is $p(y|b)$, and the green pdf is $p(y|c)$. These three curves are normalized versions of the three cross-section curves from Figure 18.

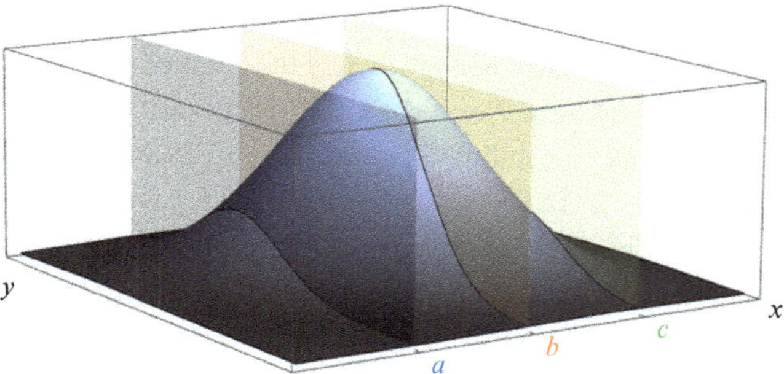

Figure 20 Conditional densities for the Gaussian pdf from Figure 15. This figure depicts the unnormalized cross-section curves. To convert the cross-section curves into pdfs, we divide by a normalization constant. The normalized curves are depicted in Figure 21.

for two other possible values *b* and *c* of *X*. Figures 20 and 21 depict the same procedure, this time applied to the pdf from Figure 15. See Section A6 for full mathematical details.

3 Bayesian Decision Theory

Bayesian decision theory studies an idealized agent who assigns credences to hypotheses. Bayesians claim that the agent's credences should conform to the probability calculus axioms. Thus, the axioms figure as norms. Bayesians supplement the probability calculus axioms with two additional norms: *Conditionalization*, which governs how credences change in response to new

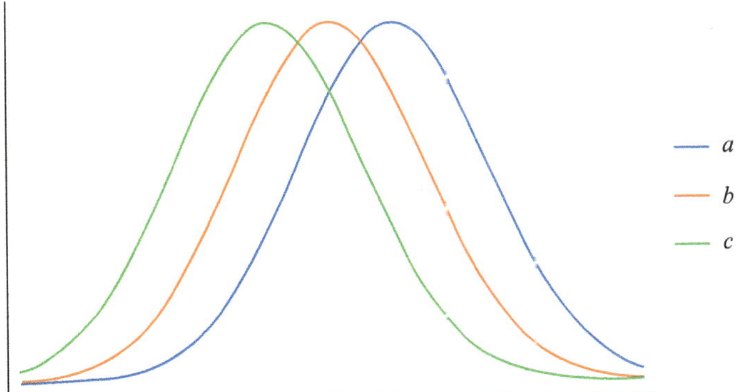

Figure 21 The one-dimensional pdfs over Y induced by Figure 20. The blue pdf is $p(y|a)$, the orange pdf is $p(y|b)$, and the green pdf is $p(y|c)$.

evidence; and *expected utility maximization*, which governs how credences guide decision-making. I discuss Conditionalization in Sections 3.1–3.2 and expected utility maximization in Section 3.3.

3.1 Conditionalization

Credences evolve. If I learn that Seabiscuit is sick, then I should lower my credence that he will win the race. Intuitively, this is because I have a relatively low credence that Seabiscuit will win the race *given that he is sick*. More generally, suppose that I begin with credence $P(H)$ and then learn E. To *conditionalize* on E is to replace my former credence $P(H)$ with $P(H|E)$. My old conditional credence $P(H|E)$ becomes my new unconditional credence in H. $P(H)$ is called the *prior probability* and $P(H|E)$ is called the *posterior probability*. We may write

$$P_{new}(H) = P(H|E),$$

to signify that my new credence in H is equal to my old conditional credence in H given E.

The intuitive idea behind the rational norm Conditionalization is that, when I receive new evidence E, I should form new credences given by

$$P_{new}(H) = P(H|E).$$

There is considerable variation in how philosophers formulate Conditionalization, depending partly upon how they gloss "new evidence." In Rescorla (2021b), I review some options and give my own preferred formulation. For present purposes, I remain as neutral as possible among alternative formulations.

However exactly we formulate Conditionalization, it is a *diachronic norm*: it governs the evolution of credences over time. In contrast, the probability calculus axioms are purely *synchronic*: they govern credences at a moment of time. Note also that we must sharply distinguish between conditionalization *the operation* and Conditionalization *the rational norm*. The former is something an agent does: revise her credences a certain way. The latter is a rational norm that requires an agent to perform the operation in certain circumstances.

As with the probability calculus axioms, there is a large literature on *why* agents should conform to Conditionalization (Greaves & Wallace, 2006; Lewis, 1999; Rescorla, 2022; Skyrms, 1987; Weisberg, 2009). Why is someone who conforms to Conditionalization rationally superior to someone who violates it? Obviously, the answer may depend on how exactly one formulates Conditionalization. In what follows, I will simply assume that Conditionalization *as formulated some way* is a rational constraint upon credal evolution.

I have focused thus far on Conditionalization in cases where $P(E) > 0$, so that the ratio formula applies. When $P(E) = 0$, the ratio formula is not well-defined. An agent who wants to conditionalize in such cases must look beyond the ratio formula for the needed conditional probabilities. For many applications, the theory of conditional densities suffices. To illustrate, suppose the agent begins with credences given by a pdf $p(x,y)$. If she receives evidence that random variable X has value x, then she can conditionalize using the conditional density $p(y|x)$. Her new credences over random variable Y are then determined by $p(y|x)$. For example, suppose the agent begins with credences given by the pdf from Figure 12 and subsequently learns X's value. If she learns that X has value a, then conditionalization leads her to new credences over Y depicted by the blue curve from Figure 19. If she instead learns that X has value b, then her new credences over Y are given by the orange curve. If she learns that X has value c, then her credences over Y are given by the green curve. In this manner, the theory of conditional densities helps us generalize Conditionalization beyond cases where $P(E) > 0$.

3.2 Bayes's Theorem

Bayesian decision theory is so-called because it assigns a central role to a theorem first proved by Bayes. The theorem states that

$$P(H|E) = \frac{P(H)P(E|H)}{P(E)}. \tag{1}$$

Equation (1) expresses the posterior probability $P(H|E)$ in terms of the prior probability $P(H)$ and the *prior likelihood* $P(E|H)$. The denominator $P(E)$

serves mainly as a normalization constant to ensure that probabilities sum to 1, so it is common to write the theorem as

$$P(H|E) = k \, P(H)P(E|H), \tag{2}$$

where $k = 1/P(E)$. One can also write the theorem as:

$$P(H|E) \propto P(H)P(E|H),$$

which highlights that the posterior is proportional to the prior times the prior likelihood:

$$posterior \propto prior \times prior \; likelihood.$$

Bayes's theorem is extraordinarily useful. In many situations, there is a natural prior probability and a natural prior likelihood. The theorem then tells us how to compute the posterior from the priors. See Section A7 for a proof of Bayes's Theorem.

Bayes's theorem must be sharply distinguished from Conditionalization. Bayes's theorem is a direct consequence of the probability calculus axioms and the ratio formula. As such, it is purely *synchronic*: it governs the relation between an agent's current conditional and unconditional credences. In contrast, Conditionalization is a *diachronic* norm. It governs how the agent's credences at an earlier time relate to her credences at a later time. Any agent who conforms to the probability calculus axioms also conforms to Bayes's theorem, but an agent who conforms to the probability calculus axioms at each moment may violate Conditionalization. Thus, one cannot derive Conditionalization from Bayes's theorem or from the probability calculus axioms. One must articulate Conditionalization as an additional constraint upon credal evolution.

That being said, Conditionalization and Bayes's theorem work together beautifully. An agent who wants to conditionalize can use Bayes's theorem to compute the posterior $P(H|E)$ and then adopt $P(H|E)$ as her new credence in H. Her new credence in H will be higher to the extent that she already assigned high credence to H and to the extent that H renders her new evidence E more likely.[4]

When $P(E) = 0$, (1) is not well-defined because the denominator is 0. Sometimes, though, a generalized analogue to (1) prevails. When a two-dimensional pdf $p(x,y)$ exists, one can prove:

$$p(x|y) = k \, p(x)p(y|x), \tag{3}$$

---

[4] In the scientific literature, the phrase "Bayes's Rule" is used sometimes to denote Conditionalization, sometimes to denote Bayes's theorem, and sometime to denote an admixture of the two.

where k is again a normalization constant. $p(x)$ serves as a *prior density*: it codifies an agent's initial credences over random variable X. $p(y|x)$ is a density for random variable Y conditional on X having value x. $p(x|y)$ is a density for X conditional on Y having value y: it serves as a *posterior density*. We may rewrite (3) as:

$$p(x|y) \propto p(x)p(y|x). \tag{4}$$

This is the form of Bayes's theorem most commonly used in scientific applications, including within Bayesian cognitive science.

We obtain a helpful visualization of (4) by holding y fixed and regarding $p(y|x)$ as a function solely of x. Viewed in this way, $p(y|x)$ is called the *likelihood function* or sometimes just the *likelihood*. Intuitively, the likelihood is an initial attempt at forming a probability density over x. The initial attempt takes into account evidence y but *not* the prior information encoded by $p(x)$.[5] Bayes's theorem tells us how to combine the initial attempt $p(y|x)$ with the prior $p(x)$, yielding the posterior density $p(x|y)$. Figures 22 and 23 illustrate. In both figures, the posterior is a compromise between the prior and the likelihood. In Figure 22, the likelihood is wide, so the posterior remains fairly close to the prior. In Figure 23, the likelihood is narrow, so it pulls the posterior far from the prior. For example, suppose that $p(y|x)$ is the conditional density of measuring speed y given that the asteroid has speed x. Assuming noisy but unbiased measurement, the likelihood peaks at y. If measurements are very noisy, then the likelihood is wide (Figure 22), and the prior over asteroid speed exerts more influence on the posterior. If measurements are less noisy, then the likelihood is narrow (Figure 23), and the prior exerts less influence.

3.3 Expected Utility Maximization

The final key notion of Bayesian decision theory is *utility*: a numerical measure of how much an agent desires an outcome. According to Bayesians, agents should choose actions that maximize *expected utility*. The expected utility of action a is a weighted average of utilities assigned to possible outcomes, where the weights are probabilities contingent upon performance of a. There are protracted debates about how to formulate expected utility maximization more rigorously (Steele & Stefánsson,

---

[5] The likelihood is not generally a pdf because the area under the curve need not be 1. However, one can always normalize and convert the likelihood into a pdf, so we can regard the likelihood as an "unnormalized" pdf.

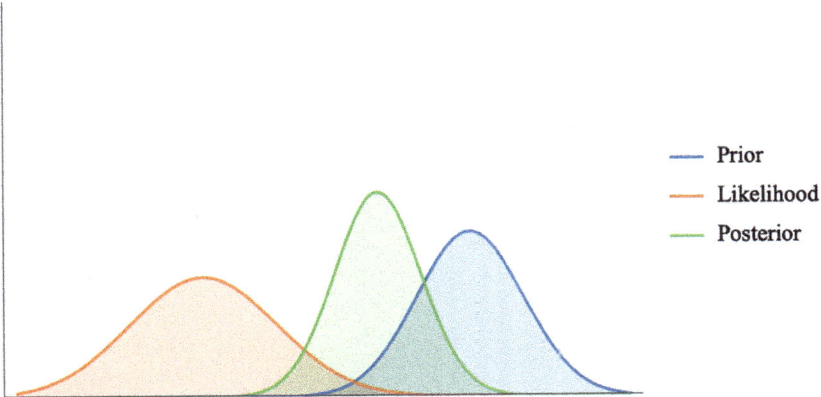

Figure 22 The likelihood peaks at the measured value y. The posterior mean is intermediate between the prior mean and y. Intuitively, the posterior is a compromise between the likelihood and the prior.

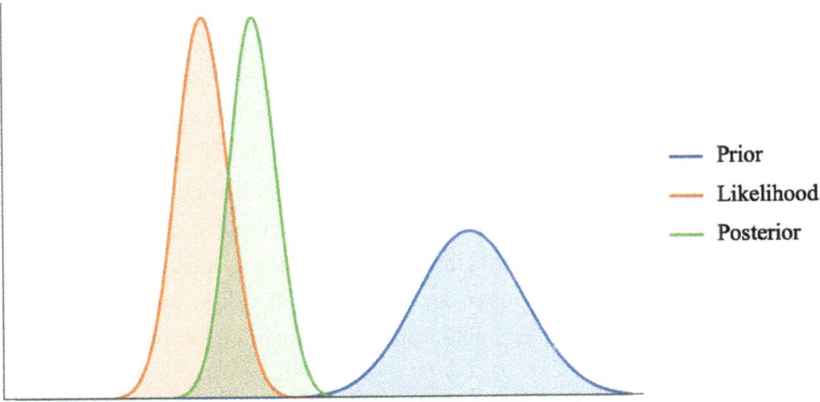

Figure 23 The prior is the same as in Figure 22. The likelihood once again peaks at y but is narrower. As a result, the posterior is narrower and is pulled closer to the likelihood. In the asteroid example, a narrower likelihood corresponds to a case where speed measurements are less noisy. It makes intuitive sense that less noisy measurements would exert more influence.

2016). We may leave it at an intuitive level. Scientific applications often deal not with utility but instead with *cost* or *loss*. The goal is then not to *maximize* expected utility but to *minimize* expected cost. For most purposes, there is no substantive difference between a utility-based formulation and a cost-based formulation: one converts a utility function into a loss function by adding a minus sign, and vice-versa.

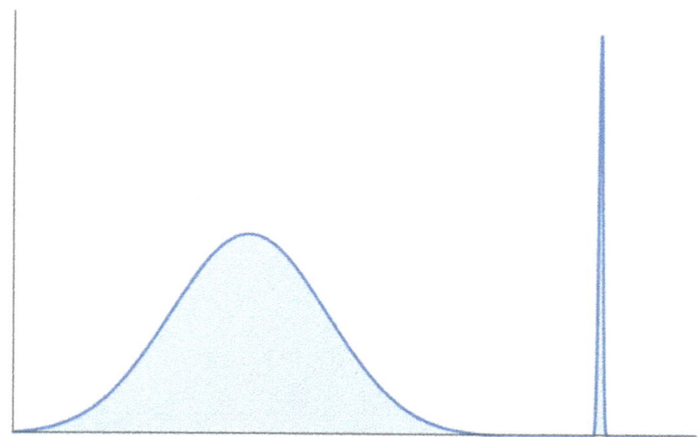

Figure 24 A pdf where most probability mass lies far from the mode.

In many statistical applications, the "action" is to estimate the value of a random variable. The standard procedure is to choose a utility function that favors selection of the true value and penalizes selection of other values. Often, selecting a best estimate will amount to selecting the *mode* of the posterior density, i.e. the value of x that maximizes the posterior density. There are also cases where the best estimate differs from the mode. If the utility function rewards estimates that are close to the true value but distinct from it, then the best estimate may be quite distant from the mode if enough probability mass lies away from the mode. Figure 24 illustrates: the mode is located in a region of relatively small probability mass; an estimator that values being close to the right answer will choose an estimate from the region of higher probability mass.

3.4 Implementation

Suppose we want a physical system (such as a computer or a robot) to implement Bayesian inference. Our first task is to decide how the system will encode credences. A major hurdle is that infinitely many distinct probabilities must often be encoded. For example, a pdf determines the probability assigned to each interval $[a, b]$. There are infinitely many such intervals. A finite physical system cannot explicitly enumerate the credence assigned to each interval. In other words, it cannot explicitly list each individual probability $P([a, b])$. After all, a finite physical system cannot explicitly list infinitely many distinct pieces of information. When credences cannot be explicitly enumerated, they must instead be *implicitly* encoded.

To illustrate implicit encoding, consider the class of Gaussian distributions. Look again at Figure 10. As noted in Section 2.4, a Gaussian distribution is completely described by two numbers: its mean and its variance. For that reason, a physical system can encode a Gaussian distribution by recording its mean m and its variance σ^2. This is an example of *parametric encoding*: the physical system encodes parameters that determine a probability distribution. The system does not explicitly enumerate the credence attaching to each interval $[a, b]$—that would be impossible. Instead, the system records two numbers (m and σ^2) that determine the credence attached to each interval $[a, b]$.

Parametric encoding is an option when the probability distribution is finitely parametrizable, which is often but not always. A more generally applicable encoding strategy features *sampling*. To illustrate, consider a physical system that draws samples stochastically from the outcome space Ω. There is an objective chance that the sampled outcome belongs to event A. We may summarize objective chances through a function:

$$Ch(A),$$

where $Ch(A)$ is the objective chance that the physical system draws an outcome belonging to A. The key idea behind sampling encoding is that these objective chances can encode subjective probabilities (Icard, 2016). The subjective probability assigned to A is simply the objective chance that a sample belongs to A:

$$P(A) = Ch(A).$$

The system encodes *subjective* probabilities via the *objective* probabilities governing its sampling activity.

Parametric and sampling encoding are widely used in statistics (Gelman et al., 2014), machine learning (Murphy, 2023), and other fields that employ the Bayesian framework.

The next crucial task is to address computation of the posterior. In some special cases, it is easy to compute the posterior from the priors. For example, when the prior probability and the likelihood are Gaussian, the posterior is also Gaussian, and its mean and variance are easily computable from those of the prior and the likelihood. Special cases aside, computing the posterior may require resources of time and memory beyond those available to a realistic agent (Kwisthout et al., 2011). Look again at Bayes's theorem (2). Multiplying $P(H)$ and $P(E|H)$ is easy. The normalization constant k is another matter. It is possible *in principle* to compute k from the prior probability and the prior likelihood, but the computation requires evaluating a (potentially very long) sum of numbers.[6] In practice, it may be impossible to compute k exactly. A similar point applies to (3). Although k is *in*

---

[6] Let $H_1, \ldots, H_n$ be a collection of disjoint events whose union is Ω. The *law of total probability*, a theorem of the probability calculus, states that $P(E) = \sum_n P(E\,H_n)P(H_n)$.

principle computable from $p(x)$ and $p(y|x)$, the computation may be impossible in practice.

A computation is *tractable* when it can be executed by a physical system with limited time and memory at its disposal. A computation is *intractable* when it is not tractable. These definitions can be made mathematically precise, but the present level of precision suffices for our purposes. The previous paragraph may be summarized as follows: computation of the posterior is not always tractable.[7]

The standard solution in Bayesian statistics is to find tractable algorithms that *approximately* implement Bayesian inference. Even when we cannot exactly compute the posterior, we can often come quite close—close enough for practical purposes. Even when we cannot conform to the normative ideal enshrined by Bayesian decision theory, we can often tractably approximate the normative ideal.

One popular approximation strategy is called *Markov chain Monte Carlo* (Murphy, 2023, pp. 493–536). MCMC algorithms use sampling to encode a credal assignment that approximates the posterior. An MCMC algorithm for approximating the posterior proceeds in discrete time stages:

$$t_1, \ t_2, \ t_3, \ldots, \ t_n, \ldots$$

At each stage, a single sample is drawn. Sampling behavior at each stage is governed by an objective chance distribution. Thus, we have a sequence of objective chance distributions:

$$Ch_1(A), \ Ch_2(A), \ Ch_3(A), \ldots, \ Ch_n(A), \ldots$$

$Ch_1(A)$ is the objective chance at time t_1 of sampling an outcome that belongs to A. $Ch_2(A)$ is the objective chance at time t_2 of sampling an outcome that belongs to A. $Ch_n(A)$ is the objective chance at time t_n of sampling an outcome that belongs to A. Objective chances evolve as the algorithm proceeds, converging asymptotically to the posterior: as the algorithm proceeds, $Ch_n(A)$ grows ever closer to the posterior probability assigned to A. After enough time has passed, the system's sampling behavior approximates the posterior quite well. See Figures 25 and 26. There are general convergence results ensuring that, in a wide range of cases, objective chances fairly quickly approach posterior probabilities (Brooks et al., 2011).

---

[7] *Computational complexity theory* studies the distinction between tractable and intractable computation. See van Rooij et al. (2019) for general discussion of computational complexity theory in relation to cognitive science.

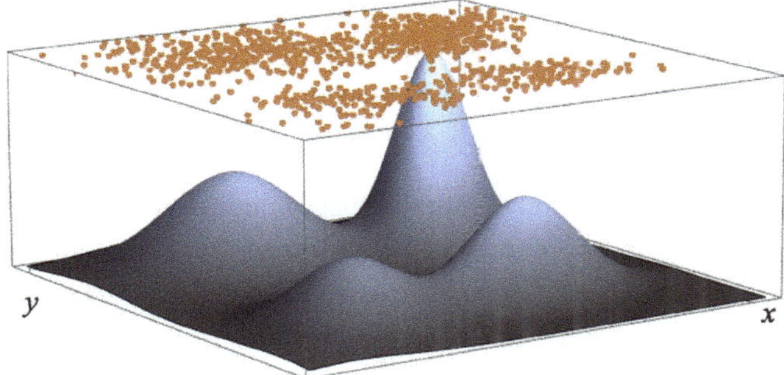

Figure 25 An illustration of MCMC approximation, for the pdf from Figure 12. The orange dots are samples in the (x, y) plane. Samples cluster in regions of high probability.

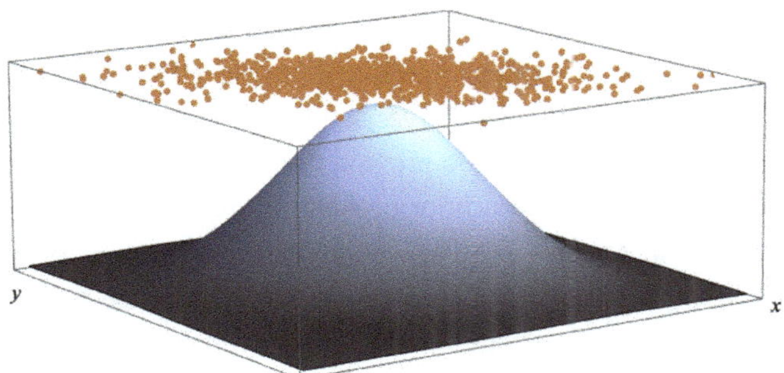

Figure 26 An illustration of MCMC approximation, for the Gaussian pdf from Figure 15.

4 Bayesian Cognitive Science

Bayesian decision theory studies how agents *should* reason and make decisions. Over the past few decades, cognitive scientists have increasingly used the Bayesian framework to describe *actual* mental activity (usually human, sometimes nonhuman). The core conjecture is that the mind copes with uncertainty by allocating credence over a hypothesis space. Credences evolve in response to sensory input, and they underwrite such tasks as estimation and decision-making. Credal activity conforms, at least approximately, to Bayesian norms.

Some Bayesian models posit exact Bayesian inference. Other models posit tractable approximations to the Bayesian ideal. I will discuss models of both kinds. I emphasize three domains where the Bayesian research program strikes me as particularly noteworthy: *perception* (Section 4.1), *motor control* (Section 4.2), and *navigation* (Section 4.3).[8]

4.1 Perception

How does the perceptual system estimate distal conditions based upon proximal sensory input? For example, how does it estimate the shapes, sizes, and locations of nearby objects based upon retinal stimulations? Proximal sensory stimulations underdetermine distal conditions: numerous possible distal conditions can cause the same proximal stimulations. Moreover, sensory input is corrupted by noise during both transduction and transmission to the brain. Despite ambiguous and noisy sensory input, the perceptual system typically forms highly accurate estimates of distal conditions.

Helmholtz (1867/1925) proposed that the perceptual system estimates distal conditions through an *unconscious inference*. Bayesian perceptual psychology develops Helmholtz's proposal, postulating unconscious Bayesian inferences executed by the perceptual system (Knill & Richards, 1996; Vilares & Kording, 2011; Rescorla, 2015a). A typical Bayesian model estimates a specific variable (e.g. shape) based on one or more proximal sensory cues (e.g. shading). The perceptual system starts with a prior probability over the distal variable and a prior likelihood that relates the distal variable to proximal sensory input. Upon receiving sensory input, the perceptual system computes the posterior (or an approximation to the posterior) over the distal variable. On that basis, the perceptual system forms a privileged estimate of distal conditions. In most Bayesian models, the estimate is chosen through expected utility maximization. In other models, the privileged estimate is chosen not deterministically but stochastically. For example, the model from (Mamassian, Landy & Maloney, 2002) implements *probability matching*: estimates are chosen stochastically, with objective probability matching the posterior.

A simple example of the Bayesian approach concerns *perceptual estimation of shape from shading*. As Figure 27 illustrates, shading is an ambiguous cue to shape. In principle, the stimulus on the left could result from a convex object lit from overhead or a concave object lit from below. Despite the ambiguity, we perceive the stimulus on the left as convex and the stimulus on the right as concave. How does the perceptual system estimate shape based upon the ambiguous evidence provided by shading? The dominant theory in perceptual psychology has long been that the perceptual system somehow "assumes" that

---

[8] Readers seeking a more comprehensive overview of the empirical literature might consult (Griffiths, Kemp & Tenenbaum, 2008), (Chater & Oaksford, 2008), or (Ma, Kording & Goldreich, 2023).

Figure 27 Shading is an ambiguous cue to shape. The stimulus on the left could result from a convex object lit from overhead or a concave object lit from below. The perceptual system "assumes" that light comes from overhead, so we perceive the stimulus on the left as convex and the stimulus on the right as concave. Reprinted from https://commons.wikimedia.org/wiki/File:%27Light-from-above%27_prior.jpg, under Creative Commons Attribution-Share Alike 4.0 International license.

light comes from overhead rather than below (Rittenhouse, 1786). This theory translates naturally into a Bayesian setting. On a Bayesian approach, the perceptual system estimates shape based on a prior over shapes, a prior over lighting directions, and a prior likelihood that assigns a probability to a given shading pattern *conditional on the stimulus having a given shape and the light coming from a given direction* (Stone, 2011). The prior over lighting directions favors overhead lighting directions. Consequently, the posterior favors the convex interpretation of the left-hand stimulus from Figure 27.

Bayesian models often posit that, when the perceptual system estimates the value of distal variable X, the prior over X has a pdf $p(x)$. Models often also posit that the prior likelihood for sensory variable Y given X has a conditional density $p(y|x)$. Upon receiving sensory input y, the perceptual system forms new credences determined by a density $p_{new}(x)$. In some models, new credences are given by the posterior density:

$$p_{new}(x) = p(x|y).$$

In other models, new credences only approximate the posterior:

$$p_{new}(x) \approx p(x|y) \ .$$

Based on $p_{new}(x)$, the perceptual system selects an estimate x^* of X's value. See Figure 28.

The motion estimation model given by Weiss, Simoncelli, and Adelson (2002) is a good example of Bayesian perceptual psychology's explanatory power. The model estimates the velocity of a moving stimulus. The model posits a prior density $p(v)$ over velocities. Crucially, the prior favors slow speeds. This reflects the environmental regularity that objects usually move fairly slowly. The model also posits a likelihood $p(I|v)$, where I measures light intensity over the retina. Upon receiving input I, the perceptual system computes the posterior $p(v|I)$ and on that basis forms a privileged velocity estimate v^*. The model explains an array of illusions that had previously resisted unified explanation. For example, it explains why low contrast stimuli seem to move slower than high contrast stimuli: low contrast stimuli yield a wide likelihood, so the "slow speed" prior exerts more influence over the posterior. See Figure 29. As this example illustrates, Bayesian perceptual models can often explain perceptual phenomena that otherwise elude satisfying explanation.

Subsequent research has further illuminated the "slow speed" prior and its crucial role in motion perception (e.g. Stocker & Simoncelli, 2006). In a particularly notable contribution, Kwon, Tadin, and Knill (2015) generalized the "slow speed" prior to construct a highly successful model of object-tracking. For further discussion of the motion estimation model, see Rescorla (2015a); Rescorla (2018b). For further discussion of the object-tracking model, see Rescorla (2020c).

Another successful application of Bayesian perceptual modeling is *cue combination*. The perceptual system typically estimates a single distal variable based on multiple cues, such as visual and haptic cues to size. Due to sensory

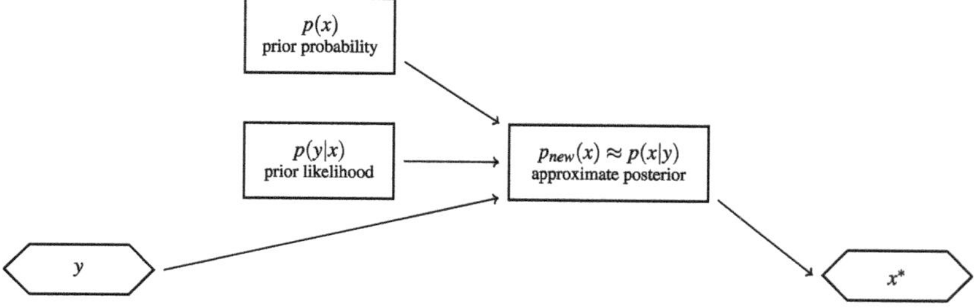

Figure 28 Approximate Bayesian inference in the perceptual system. When $p_{new}(x) = p(x|y)$, inference is exact rather than approximate.

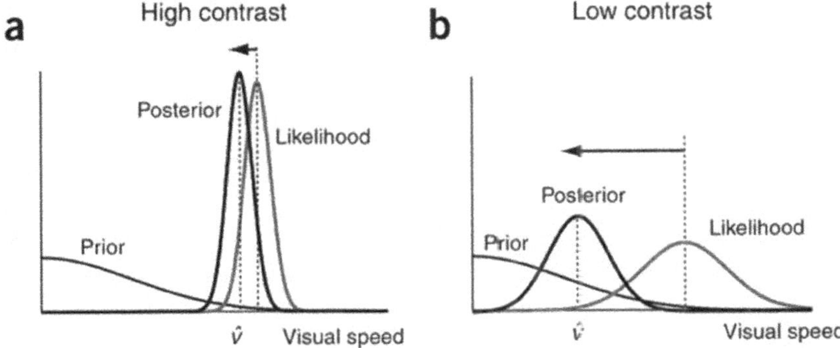

Figure 29 Illustrates how the "slow speed" prior influences motion estimation. When the stimulus has high contrast, the likelihood is narrow and the "slow speed" prior exerts relatively little influence on the posterior. When the stimulus has low contrast, the likelihood is wide and the prior exerts relatively more influence on the posterior. v̂, the posterior mean, is smaller in the low contrast condition (b) than in the high contrast condition (a). Reprinted with permission from Springer Nature Customer Service Center GmbH: Springer Nature, *Nature*, "Noise Characteristics and Prior Expectations in Human Visual Perception" (Stocker & Simoncelli, 2006).

noise, estimates based on distinct sensory cues will typically differ at least to a small degree. The perceptual system must combine distinct sensory cues into a single unified estimate of the distal variable. Ernst and Banks (2002) showed that the Bayesian framework can successfully model combination of visual and haptic cues to size. Researchers have subsequently generalized this finding to numerous other cases of cue combination within and across modalities (Trommershäuser, Kording & Landy, 2011). See Rescorla (2020b) for further discussion of cue combination in a Bayesian setting.

Bayesian perceptual inference is subpersonal and inaccessible to conscious introspection or control. These inferences are executed *by the perceptual system*, not by the *perceiver*. A typical perceiver is not aware that her perceptual system uses a "slow speed" prior. The perceptual system, not the perceiver, encodes and deploys the prior. The perceiver is not consciously aware of any inference based on the prior.

Perceptual priors are highly mutable, changing rapidly in response to altered environmental statistics. Adams, Graf, and Ernst (2004) exposed subjects to deviant visual-haptic input indicating an altered lighting direction. In response, shape perception and lightness perception rapidly changed, reflecting a change in the "light from overhead" prior. Similarly, the "slow speed" prior rapidly changes in response to fast-moving stimuli (Sotiroupolous, Seitz & Seriès, 2011).

There is also evidence that prior likelihoods are mutable (Sato & Kording, 2014; Sato, Toyoizumi & Aihara, 2007; Seydell, Knill & Trommershäuser, 2010). Changing priors can themselves be modeled in Bayesian terms (Kwon & Knill, 2013).

As final illustration of Bayesian perceptual psychology's explanatory power, consider *central tendency bias*: perceptual estimates of a magnitude are biased towards the mean of the sample distribution (Hollingworth, 1910). Relatively large magnitudes tend to be underestimated, while relatively small magnitudes tend to be overestimated. Depending on the case, the sample distribution may arise naturally or may be experimentally imposed. Central tendency bias is a ubiquitous effect, arising when subjects estimate line length (Duffy et al., 2010), interval duration (Jazayeri & Shadlen, 2010), color (Olkkonen, McCarthy & Allred, 2014), and many other magnitudes. It is readily explicable from a Bayesian perspective. The key posit is that the prior adapts to match environmental statistics. For example, when the subject encounters stimuli drawn from an experimentally imposed sample distribution, the prior shifts to match that distribution. The shifted prior pulls estimates towards the prior mean. See Figure 30. Researchers have elaborated this intuitive idea into models that successfully explain central tendency bias for a number of perceptual tasks (Glasauer, 2019; Glasauer & Shi, 2022; Petzschner, Glasauer & Stephan, 2015). The models achieve a close fit with psychophysical data, including detailed patterns governing the extent to which central tendency bias occurs in different situations.

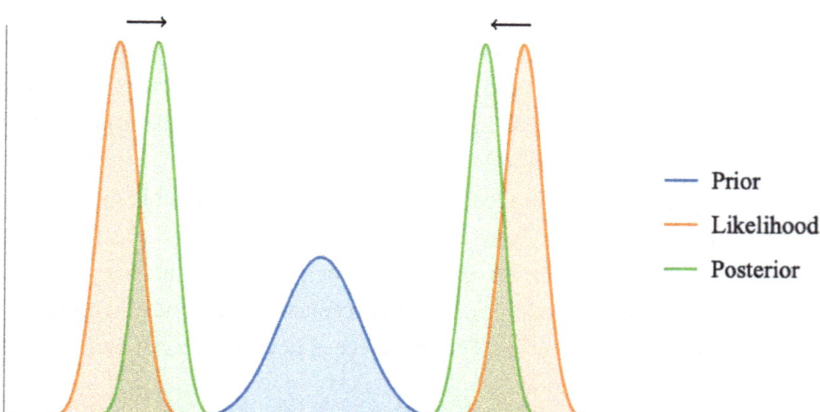

Figure 30 Heuristic Bayesian explanation of central tendency bias. Two possible likelihoods are depicted: the first peaks below the prior mean, and the second peaks above the prior mean. In both cases, the posterior mean is pulled towards the prior mean. Assuming that the prior is adapted to the sample distribution, the posterior mean exhibits central tendency bias.

In summary, Bayesian modeling has proved remarkably successful across a range of perceptual tasks. It amply deserves its orthodox status within contemporary perceptual psychology.

4.2 Motor Control

Suppose I form an intention to perform an action, such as lifting a coffee cup without spillage. My motor system must convert my intention into *motor commands* that promote fulfillment of my intention. As Bernstein (1967) emphasized, the motor system has multiple degrees of freedom when converting intentions into motor commands. For example, there are infinitely many possible hand trajectories through which I can lift the coffee cup without spillage. The motor system must select among these infinitely many options.

Sensorimotor psychology studies how the motor system selects motor commands that promote the agent's goals. Over the past few decades, Bayesian models have achieved great explanatory success within sensorimotor psychology (Haith & Krakauer, 2013; Shadmehr & Mussa-Ivaldi, 2012). *Optimal feedback control* (OFC) models have proved especially successful (Todorov 2004; Todorov & Jordan, 2002). OFC models have two core elements: an *estimator*, which uses conditionalization to estimate current environmental conditions (including bodily state); and a *controller*, which uses expected cost minimization to select suitable motor commands.

When the controller issues a motor command u, it sends an *efference copy* of the motor command back to the estimator. The efference copy serves as input to a *forward model* (Wolpert & Flanagan, 2009). Intuitively, the forward model reflects how bodily state will change due to motor commands. More rigorously, it encodes conditional densities $p(x_{t+1}|x_t, u)$, where x_t is bodily state at time t, u is a motor command, and x_{t+1} is bodily state at time $t + 1$. Using efference copy and the forward model, the estimator forms an initial probabilistic estimate of bodily state. Since motor execution is noisy, the initial estimate requires *sensory correction*. For example, an initial probabilistic estimate of hand position can be revised based upon visual and proprioceptive feedback regarding hand position. The estimator sequentially updates credences over environmental conditions based upon sequentially received efference copy and sensory feedback.

Throughout performance of the motor task, the controller uses updated credences to compute expected costs of possible motor commands. A cost function $c(h, u)$ reflects the cost of motor command u assuming that outcome h is the true outcome. During a reaching task, h might specify hand position,

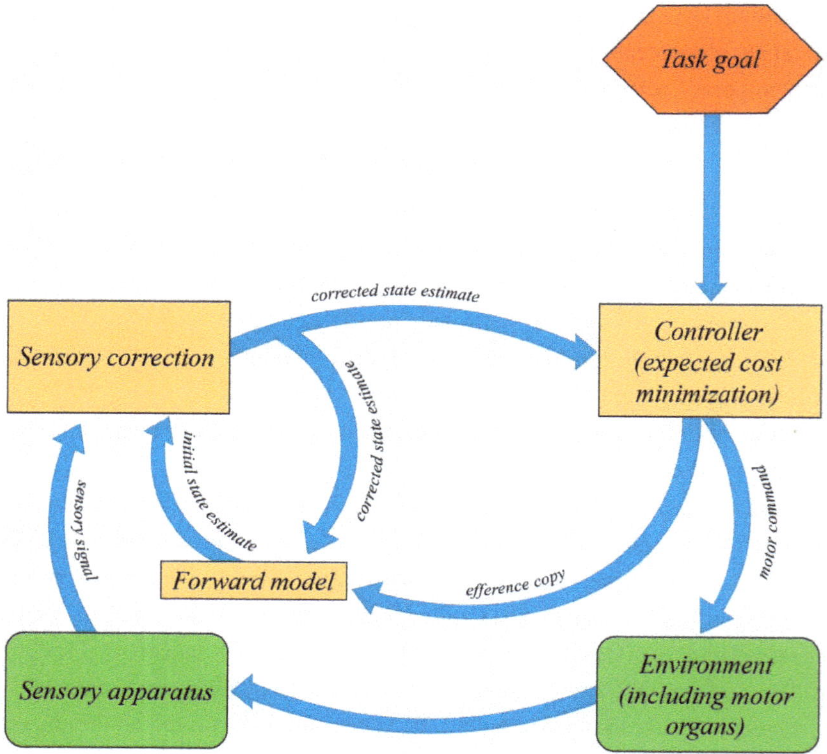

Figure 31 A template for Bayesian models of sensorimotor control. Some models vary the template somewhat. For example, the Saunders & Knill (2004) model handles sensory delay by transmitting the initial state estimate rather than the corrected state estimate to the controller. Modified from Rescorla (2016) with permission from John Wiley & Sons.

hand velocity, and the target location. Typically, the cost function has two components. The first component, which is task-dependent, rewards achievement of the task goal (e.g. reaching the target). The second component, which is task-independent, penalizes energetic expenditure. At every stage, the controller selects a motor command that minimizes expected costs. See Figure 31.

OFC models of motor control have achieved great empirical success (McNamee & Wolpert, 2019). Most notably, OFC explains patterns in repeated performance of a task. When a subject repeatedly executes a task, the movement details vary across trials. As Bernstein (1967) first showed, and as subsequent research has amply confirmed, movement details vary more along *task-irrelevant* dimensions than *task-relevant* dimensions. The discrepancy between task-relevant variation and task-irrelevant variation is

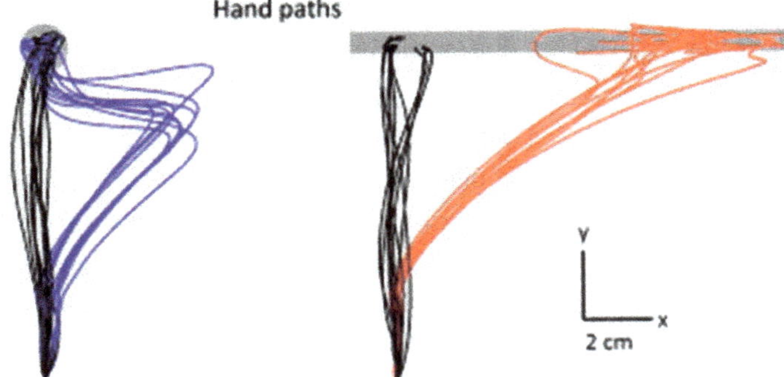

Figure 32 Subjects reached either to a circle or a rectangle. Unperturbed hand paths are shown in black. In some trials, hand trajectories were perturbed to the right. How the motor system responded depended upon the task goal: the motor system corrected trajectories when reaching for the circle but not when reaching for the rectangle. In other words, it corrected task-relevant perturbations but not task-irrelevant perturbations. Reprinted from Scott (2012) with permission from Elsevier.

one of the most robust findings in sensorimotor psychology, surfacing in a huge range of motor tasks. The discrepancy is readily explicable within the OFC framework (Todorov & Jordan, 2002). Whenever bodily trajectory is perturbed (e.g. by noise or by an external influence), the controller must choose whether to correct the perturbation or leave it uncorrected. Correcting the perturbation expends energy, so an optimal controller will only correct perturbations that are task-relevant. As a result, deviations from the average trajectory accumulate along task-irrelevant dimensions but not task-relevant dimensions.

An experiment conducted by Nashed, Crevecoeur, and Scott (2012) nicely illustrates the contrasting response to task-relevant and task-irrelevant perturbations. Subjects reached quickly to a target: either a relatively small circle or else a relatively wide rectangle. In some trials, an external force disrupted the reaching motion. When the target was the circle, the external disruption was task-relevant, so the motor system corrected for it. When the target was the rectangle, the external disruption was task-irrelevant, so the motor system did not correct for it. See Figure 32.[9]

Priors deployed during motor control are mutable (Berniker, Voss & Kording, 2010; Fernandes et al., 2014). Consider a study conducted by Kording and

---

[9] For further discussion of Bayesian sensorimotor psychology, with an emphasis on OFC, see Rescorla (2016); Rescorla (2019). See also Burge (2022, pp. 502–530).

Wolpert (2004). Subjects reached to a visible target in a virtual reality setup. Finger position was hidden during the reaching motion, except that subjects received visual feedback on finger position midway through the motion. Apparent finger position was shifted from actual finger position, with the shift drawn randomly from a prior distribution (a Gaussian distribution for some subjects, a bimodal distribution for other subjects). The motor system learned the experimentally imposed prior (either the Gaussian prior or the bimodal prior) and used it to adjust finger trajectories based on visual feedback.

4.3 Navigation

Animal navigation has been intensively studied for many decades across several disciplines, including psychology, ethology, and neuroscience. At present, Bayesian modeling does not figure as prominently in the study of navigation as it does in perceptual psychology and sensorimotor psychology. Nevertheless, recent studies provide strong evidence that Bayesian inference plays a crucial role in human navigation.

I focus on a navigational strategy called *dead reckoning*. During dead reckoning, the navigator exploits self-motion cues to maintain a running estimate of her own position. Self-motion cues include optic flow, efference copy, vestibular signals, and so on. Dead reckoning is sometimes called "path integration," because position is the integral of velocity. Dead reckoning pervades the animal kingdom (Gallistel, 1990, pp. 57–102), from the desert ant to humans.

A key fact about human dead reckoning is that, in many experimental conditions, subjects overshoot the target destination. Traditionally, overshooting was explained through a "leaky integrator" model (Lappe et al., 2011). The basic idea is that subjects imperfectly integrate velocity to compute position: rather than computing the true integral, subjects compute a slightly smaller quantity. As the distance traveled increases, "leaks" accumulate and the discrepancy between estimated position and true position increases. Lakshminarasimhan et al. (2018) offer an alternative Bayesian explanation. They posit a "slow speed" prior over self-motion. The "slow speed" prior biases estimated velocity below the true velocity, which leads the subject to underestimate distance traveled. See Figure 33.

The "slow speed" model explains several phenomena that the "leaky integrator" model does not. For example, Lakshminarasimhan et al. (2018) studied dead reckoning in a virtual reality setup. They manipulated the optic flow cue by altering the density of plane elements: greater density entails a more reliable cue. Decreased cue reliability corresponds to a relatively wide likelihood. The "slow speed" model predicts that, when the likelihood is wide, the posterior will

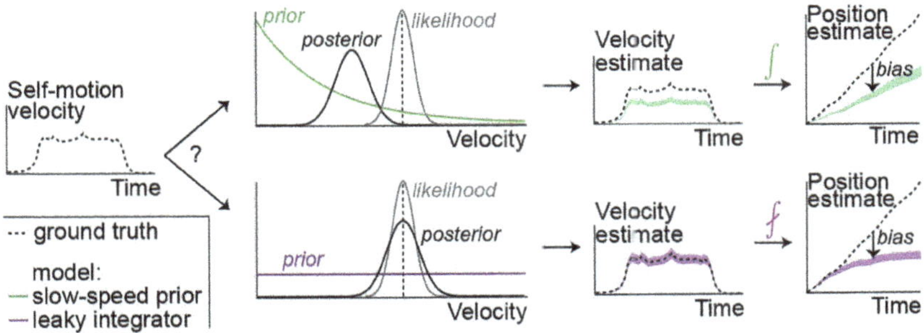

Figure 33 Comparison of the "slow speed" prior model and a "leaky integrator" model. (For heuristic purposes, the comparison only depicts one-dimensional linear velocity. The actual model also considers angular velocity.) The panel on the left shows the subject's true velocity over time. The top row schematizes the "slow speed" prior model. At a given moment, the "slow speed" prior (in green) combines with the likelihood to yield a posterior over possible velocities. The resulting velocity estimates are consistently smaller than actual velocity, due to the influence of the "slow speed" prior. When velocity estimates are integrated to form position estimates, the position estimates are biased. The bottom panel shows a Bayesian version of the "leaky integrator" approach. (One can also develop the "leaky integrator" approach in a non-Bayesian setting.) The prior is uniform. As a result, velocity estimates are not biased towards smaller velocities. The bias in position estimates stems from leaky integration, not from biased velocity estimates. Reprinted from (Lakshminarasimhan et al., 2018) with permission from Elsevier.

be more strongly affected by the "slow speed" prior, causing even more overshooting. In contrast, the "leaky integrator" model does not predict that a degraded optic flow cue causes increased overshooting. See Figure 34. The human data exhibited more overshooting in response to the degraded optic flow cue, conforming closely to the "slow speed" model's predictions.

Another striking phenomenon explained by the model: when the target is relatively distant, overshooting gives way to *undershooting*. The farther the subject travels, the greater the uncertainty regarding her position, so the wider her pdf over possible positions. When the pdf becomes quite wide, its area of overlap with the target decreases. As a result, expected utility peaks *before* the target when the target is relatively far away. For sufficiently large distances, this bias towards undershooting swamps the bias induced by the "slow speed" prior. The Bayesian model, by analyzing how these two biases interact with each other and with optic flow reliability, achieves a good match with actual human performance.

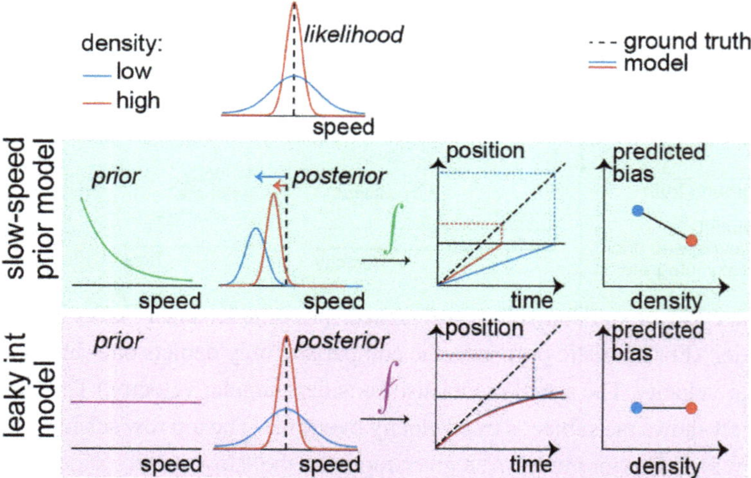

Figure 34 Differing predictions of the "slow speed" model and the "leaky integrator" model. The red likelihood function is narrow, corresponding to a reliable optic flow cue. The blue likelihood function is wide, corresponding to a degraded optic flow cue. In the "slow speed" prior model, the prior exerts more influence in degraded cases, causing a more biased position estimate. The "leaky integrator" model predicts that a change in cue reliability does not affect the position estimate. The "leaky integrator" approach is illustrated here in a Bayesian format, but the same prediction prevails for non-Bayesian versions. Reprinted from (Lakshminarasimhan et al., 2018) with permission from Elsevier.

Central tendency bias provides additional evidence for a Bayesian approach to dead reckoning. Petszchner and Glasauer (2011) studied a virtual reality task in which subjects traversed an experimentally imposed linear path and then tried to reproduce their displacement. Subjects performed the task in multiple trials during each session. Distances during a session were drawn from one of three distinct sample distributions: small, medium, or large. Subjects exhibited significant central tendency bias: their distance estimates during a session (as gauged by reproduced distance) were biased towards the mean of the session sample distribution. To explain the bias, Petszchner and Glasauer (2011) offer an iterative Bayesian model. After each trial, the Bayesian estimator updates its prior over distance traveled. The prior gravitates towards the mean of the session sample distribution, biasing distance estimates towards that mean. The model thereby explains observed central tendency bias, further confirming the hypothesis that human dead reckoning relies upon Bayesian estimation.

Dead reckoning is only one navigation strategy found in the animal kingdom. Equally important is *piloting*, during which the creature uses landmarks to estimate its own position (Gallistel, 1990, p. 41, pp. 88–93, pp. 120–123). Even relatively primitive creatures, such as rats and bats, engage in piloting. Of course, humans routinely do so. There is strong evidence that human piloting relies on Bayesian inference (Jetzschke et al., 2017), as does human combination of self-motion cues and landmark cues (Chen et al., 2017).

Dead reckoning and piloting are key to navigation, but they are just the beginning. Piloting presupposes *mapping*: estimation of landmark locations. Mapping also figures prominently in robotics, where the standard solution centers upon approximate Bayesian inference (Thrun, Burgard & Fox, 2005). Several researchers have conjectured that some mammals likewise implement Bayesian mapping (Gallistel, 2008; Rescorla, 2009). The conjecture fits well with everything we know about mammalian navigation (Savelli & Knierim, 2019; Shikauchi et al., 2021). Moreover, it can explain within a single theoretical framework disparate navigational phenomena that otherwise resist unified explanation (Kessler, Frankenstein & Rothkopf, 2024). The topic merits, and will surely receive, further investigation.

4.4 Other Psychological Domains

Researchers have applied the Bayesian perspective to numerous domains, such as *causal reasoning* (Griffiths & Tenenbaum, 2009; Oaksford & Chater, 2020), *social cognition* (Baker & Tenenbaum, 2014), *intuitive physics* (Battaglia, Hamrock & Tenenbaum, 2013; Sanborn, Masinghka & Griffiths, 2013), *language acquisition* (Abend et al., 2017), *syntactic parsing* (Narayanan & Jurafsky, 1998), *concept acquisition* (Goodman et al., 2008), *music cognition* (Temperley, 2007), *reading* (Norris, 2006), *memory* (Hemmer & Steyvers, 2009), *categorization* (Sanborn, Griffiths & Navarro, 2010), and so on. Applications vary in their predictive and explanatory power. Few achieve the astonishing explanatory successes found in perception and motor control. Still, they are often more successful than competing non-Bayesian approaches, as readers can confirm for themselves by accessing the above-cited texts.

4.5 Anti-Bayesian Phenomena?

Like every prominent cognitive science research program, Bayesian modeling has attracted lots of criticism (Bowers & Davis, 2012; Eberhardt & Danks, 2011; Jones & Love, 2011; Mandelbaum, 2019). Perhaps the most basic criticism is that many mental phenomena appear radically anti-Bayesian. This criticism traces back to Kahneman and Tversky, who discovered intriguing cognitive phenomena that apparently violate Bayesian norms (e.g. Kahneman & Tversky, 1979; Tversky & Kahneman, 1983). A good example is *anchoring bias* (Tversky & Kahneman, 1974): when asked to estimate a quantity (such as the distance between Los Angeles and San Francisco), people are *biased* towards a randomly selected number provided to them. In effect, the randomly selected number serves as an "anchor" that pulls judgment away from a more accurate estimate. Anchoring bias is irrational and hence suggests that people violate the norms of Bayesian decision theory. Beyond the cognitive-level irrationalities discovered by Kahneman and Tversky, researchers have documented seemingly anti-Bayesian phenomena in other domains, including perception (Gardner, 2019; Mandelbaum et al., 2020; Rahnev & Denison, 2018).

Proponents of Bayesian modeling reply that many apparently anti-Bayesian phenomena can in fact be modeled in Bayesian terms (Stocker, 2018). Consider the size–weight illusion: when you lift two objects of equal weight but different size, the smaller object feels heavier. At first, the illusion looks anti-Bayesian because it flouts a prior expectation that larger objects are heavier. However, the illusion turns out to be explicable by a Bayesian model that estimates relative densities (Peters et al., 2016).

Even when a phenomenon cannot be modeled in Bayesian terms, it can often be modeled in terms of *approximately* Bayesian inference (Chater et al., 2020). In this spirit, Lieder et al. (2018) show that anchoring bias arises naturally from a sampling approximation to idealized Bayesian inference. They assume that, when subjects are provided with a randomly selected number, this number serves as the initial sample for an MCMC algorithm. (See Section 3.4 to review MCMC algorithms.) Samples are biased towards the initial sample, which may be quite far from an optimal Bayesian estimate. As the algorithm proceeds, it draws samples closer to the optimal Bayesian estimate. The extent of anchoring bias depends upon how long the algorithm runs (i.e. how many samples it draws). When computation is costly (e.g. because computational resources are needed for another task), anchoring bias increases because the system draws fewer samples and does not get as far from the initial sample. On this approach, anchoring bias arises from "rational" use of limited computational resources: the system balances accurate estimation against the cost of computation. The sampling model explains a range of effects, such as increased anchoring bias due to cognitive load or time pressure. Many other seemingly anti-Bayesian cognitive phenomena can be similarly explained in terms of sampling approximation to idealized Bayesian inference (Chater et al., 2020; Dasgupta, Schulz & Gershman, 2017).

Obviously, there is no guarantee that all psychological processes will turn out to be Bayesian or approximately Bayesian. Sub-systems may conform to

Bayesian norms to a greater or lesser degree. For example, it could be that perception conforms quite closely to Bayesian norms while high-level decision-making does not. It could be that *certain* perceptual processes conform closely to Bayesian norms while other perceptual processes do not, or that certain perceptual processes conform to Bayesian norms *under certain circumstances* but not other circumstances—e.g. that perceptual processes conform to Bayesian norms only when the perceiver is paying attention (Morales et al., 2015). These possibilities require investigation. We must build and test detailed Bayesian models of specific phenomena, evaluating afresh how well each model fits the data. That is exactly what Bayesian cognitive scientists do on a daily basis. Underlying this research program is a key methodological commitment: enough mental processes are at least approximately Bayesian that constructing and testing Bayesian models of specific mental processes is a worthwhile endeavor. So far, the methodological commitment has been amply vindicated.[10]

4.6 Where do the Priors Come From?

A natural question posed by Bayesian modeling is how the prior probability and prior likelihood arise. For example, the Bayesian dead reckoning model assumes a "slow speed" prior but says nothing about the prior's etiology. A similar point applies to other Bayesian models found in the literature. The models postulate priors that underlie Bayesian inference, without explaining how the priors arise. Given that priors are highly mutable, a good explanation will surely cite a complex mixture of evolutionary and developmental factors. So far, though, no such explanation is available.

Some critics complain that Bayesian models are unexplanatory due to their reliance on postulated priors (Hutto & Myin, 2017, pp. 67–74, pp. 154–155; Orlandi, 2014, p. 91). The worry is that Bayesian models rest upon unexplained explainers. How much can a Bayesian model explain when it posits priors but offers no explanation for the priors?

---

[10] Many supposedly anti-Bayesian phenomena documented by Kahneman and Tversky (such as the *conjunction fallacy*) involve explicit probability judgments: researchers ask subjects to judge relative probabilities of various possibilities; elicited judgments violate the probability calculus axioms. Poor performance in an explicit probabilistic task is hardly evidence that the subject does not execute Bayesian inference, any more than poor performance in a symbolic logic class is evidence that a student does not execute deductive inference. Bayesian cognitive science does not claim that ordinary people are good at probability theory. It claims that ordinary people (or their psychological subsystems) assign subjective probabilities and execute Bayesian operations over the assigned probabilities. Typically, the probability assignments are not explicit but are instead implicitly encoded.

In my opinion, this complaint has no force. We must distinguish between *incomplete* theories and *unexplanatory* theories. Every scientific theory contains unexplained explainers: postulates that serve as explanantia. For example, Newtonian physics postulates that objects have mass, but it does not explain how objects come to have the masses that they have. No one should complain on that basis that Newtonian physics is unexplanatory. In many cases, a successful scientific theory contains huge explanatory gaps. A famous example is the theory of natural selection as formulated in *On The Origin of Species*. Darwin postulated suitable hereditary mechanisms but had no clue what those mechanisms were. No one should complain on that basis that the theory of natural selection as formulated by Darwin was unexplanatory. A scientific theory can offer powerful explanations even though it includes unexplained explainers.

Of course, it is always good to eliminate unexplained explainers. Modern biology achieved a decisive advance when it discovered the genetic basis of heredity. Bayesian cognitive science will likewise achieve a major advance when it illuminates the etiology of priors. Until that advance, Bayesian cognitive science will be incomplete in a significant way. Even in its present incomplete state, it offers powerful explanations for many psychological phenomena.

5 Realism and Instrumentalism

Any Bayesian model posits *credal states* (assignments of credences to hypotheses) and *credal transitions* (transitions among credal states). At a bare minimum, a Bayesian model posits a prior probability, a prior likelihood, and a transition to a posterior or approximate posterior. The Bayesian model may posit a succession of credal states, as in sensorimotor psychology.

Suppose that a Bayesian model is explanatorily successful, in the sense that it supplies compelling explanations for observed phenomena. Let us distinguish two opposing viewpoints one might adopt towards the model: *realism* and *instrumentalism*. Realists hold that we have good reason to deem the model an approximately true description of mental activity (Rescorla, 2020c). From a realist perspective, the mind instantiates credal states and transitions at least roughly like those posited by the model. The model describes actual mental states and processes that mediate between inputs (e.g. retinal inputs) and outputs (e.g. perceptual estimates; motor commands). Instrumentalists, on the other hand, regard the model as nothing but a useful predictive device (Block, 2018; Colombo & Seriès, 2012; Orlandi, 2014). The model helps us summarize the mapping (possibly stochastic) from inputs to outputs, but it does not describe actual mental states and processes with even approximate accuracy. From an instrumentalist perspective, we have no reason to believe that the mind instantiates credal states or that it executes anything resembling (approximate) Bayesian inference. We should conclude only that the mind operates *as if* it executes (approximate) Bayesian inference. Whereas realists attribute psychological reality to credal states and transitions postulated by explanatorily successful Bayesian models, instrumentalists do not.

To illustrate how realism and instrumentalism differ, consider Figure 28. The figure depicts how the perceptual system converts proximal sensory input y into a perceptual estimate x^*. It posits two mental states (the prior probability and the prior likelihood) that along with y cause a third mental state (the approximate posterior), which in turn causes perceptual estimate x^*. From a realist perspective, we should take this causal structure seriously as a guide to underlying psychological reality. There really do exist priors, they really do interact with input y to cause an approximate posterior, and this approximate posterior really does cause a perceptual estimate x^*. In contrast, instrumentalists do not take Figure 28 as a guide to underlying psychological reality. All that we should take seriously about Figure 28, they say, is the induced mapping from input y to estimate x^*.

I have defended realism at length in previous writings (Rescorla, 2015a; Rescorla, 2015b; Rescorla, 2020c). Here, I will briefly adduce a few considerations in its favor.

5.1 Scientific Realism

My realist perspective on Bayesian cognitive science is grounded in a general commitment to *scientific realism*. Scientific realism traces back to Putnam (1975) and has been elaborated by many subsequent philosophers. The basic idea is that explanatory success is a *prima facie* indication of approximate truth. When a scientific theory is explanatorily successful, we have *prima facie* reason to believe that it is at least approximately true. For example, the explanatory success of modern physics provides reason to believe in subatomic particles.

My realist perspective on Bayesian cognitive science results from straightforward application of scientific realism to Bayesian modeling. Many Bayesian models, although not all, are explanatorily successful. From a scientific realist perspective, we have reason to regard these models as at least approximately true. We have reason to accept that there exist credal states and transitions roughly like those posited by the model. Just as the explanatory success of modern physics provides reason to believe in subatomic particles, the explanatory success of a Bayesian model provides reason to believe in credal states and transitions.

Not all philosophers accept scientific realism. Some authors favor an instrumentalist perspective on scientific theorizing (van Fraassen, 1980). According to instrumentalism, a scientific theory is just a useful tool for making predictions. When a scientific theory is explanatorily successful, we have no reason to believe that the theory is even approximately true. For example, the explanatory success of modern physics provides no reason to believe that there are subatomic particles. Philosophers who favor an instrumentalist perspective more generally will surely want to apply it specifically to Bayesian cognitive science. If you do not believe in a subatomic particles, then you probably do not believe in credal states and transitions!

Typically, researchers who favor instrumentalism about Bayesian cognitive science do not evince a more general commitment to instrumentalism about scientific theorizing. They do not hold that we should be instrumentalists about scientific theories *in general*. Instead, they argue that we should be instrumentalists *for the special case of Bayesian cognitive science*. In my opinion, their arguments for that differential stance have little force. I see no compelling reason why philosophers inclined towards scientific realism *in general* should favor instrumentalism for the special case of Bayesian modeling. I will illustrate my viewpoint by critiquing an instrumentalist argument advanced by Block (2023) and tailored to the special case of Bayesian cognitive science.

5.2 Simulation or Implementation?

According to Block, we seldom if ever have reason to believe that a psychological system *implements* approximate Bayesian inference as opposed to merely *simulating* approximate Bayesian inference. To support his assessment, Block cites evolutionary considerations (2023, p. 208):

> Evolution is a pro-instrumentalist mechanism. There is no doubt that behaving according to Bayesian norms is enormously valuable for an organism and we can expect strong evolutionary pressure toward behavior that fits the norms of Bayesian rationality. But Bayesian rational behavior does not have to be implemented using the conceptual apparatus that is best suited to describing Bayesian rational processes by the theorist. The problem with Rescorla's argument is that it is not clear that the way evolution chose to produce behavior that adheres roughly to Bayesian norms involves the representation of probabilities in the perceptual system.

Block develops his position by citing an experiment on pea plants conducted by Dener, Kacelnik, and Shemesh (2016). Each plant's roots were divided between two pots. The two pots received equal mean levels of nutrients. Nutrient levels were constant in one pot and variable in the other. More roots developed in the constant pot if the mean nutrient level was high, and more roots developed in the variable pot if the mean nutrient level was low. This growth pattern comports with expected utility theory, which (assuming a suitably shaped utility function) mandates risk aversion in rich conditions and risk proneness in poor conditions. Block writes (2023, pp. 209–210):

> [T]he pea plant behaves as if it represented mean levels of nutrients and their degree of uncertainty. Since the pea plant lacks a nervous system, we can be pretty sure that there are no such representations. Somehow, natural selection has found a way for plants to behave according to some of the norms of Bayesian rationality without those representations. The challenge to Rescorla's reasoning is that we have to allow for the possibility that the same is true of *our perceptual systems*.

Block concludes that, even if we favor a realist stance towards scientific theorizing in general, we should adopt an instrumentalist stance towards Bayesian perceptual psychology. Presumably he would extend the conclusion to other branches of Bayesian cognitive science.

In evaluating Block's argument, we must carefully distinguish between subjective and objective probability. Due to the experimental protocols, there are objective probabilities that govern the nutrient level in each pot. We might gloss these either as frequencies or as chances. Either way, they are objective features of the world, lacking any subjective element. Given a pot's objective probability distribution, we can describe the mean and the variance. The experiment shows that root growth is sensitive to both the mean and the variance. Thus, root growth is sensitive to objective probabilities (or to properties that supervene upon objective probabilities).

One might try to explain that sensitivity by attributing credal states to the pea plants. One might posit *subjective* probabilities, instantiated by each plant, that track the *objective* probabilities governing each pot. One might postulate that root growth is influenced by an expected utility computation based upon the posited subjective probabilities. I agree with Block that the proposed explanation is both *implausible* and *unmotivated*. It is implausible because plant physiology does not seem able to support expected utility computations. It is unmotivated because nothing about the pea plant study indicates that credal states or utility functions mediate the causal influence of objective probabilities upon root growth. The mere fact that a system is sensitive to the mean and variance of an objective probability distribution does not suggest that the system instantiates credal states. For example, we can construct a machine whose outputs are sensitive to the frequency with which a biased coin lands heads; there is no reason why the machine must instantiate credal states. Mere sensitivity to objective probabilities (or properties that supervene on objective probabilities) is not a *prima facie* indicator of Bayesian computation. This remains so even when the mapping from objective probabilities to outputs happens to mirror the dictates of expected utility theory.

One can describe any system using Bayesian decision theory. Adapting an example of Dennett's (1987, p. 23), one can "explain" why a lectern does not move by saying that the lectern assigns high utility to occupying the optimal location in the universe and assigns high credence to the hypothesis that it currently occupies the optimal location in the universe. Clearly, though, we should not accept the purported "explanation." It contributes no value to our theorizing. It does not improve upon a non-Bayesian explanation couched wholly in terms of physics (e.g. an explanation that cites the law of inertia). A similar diagnosis applies to the pea plant study. The two cases are not totally analogous, because we know why the lectern does not move (inertia) but do not yet know the physiological mechanisms through which objective probabilities causally influence root growth. Still, as Dener, Kacelnik, and Shemesh (2016) themselves emphasize, nothing about the pea plant study suggests that the mechanisms involve credal states or utility functions. We have no reason to think that Bayesian modeling would add any explanatory force to an eventual physiological explanation couched in non-Bayesian terms.

A very different diagnosis applies to numerous Bayesian models offered in cognitive science, including but not limited to perceptual psychology. In many cases, the Bayesian model adds considerable explanatory value to our theorizing. For example, the (Lakshminarasimhan et al., 2018) dead reckoning model explains why more overshooting occurs when the optic flow cue is degraded, and it *also* explains why undershooting occurs for relatively distant targets. The model thereby achieves the unity characteristic of good explanation. Similarly, the (Weiss, Simoncelli & Adelson, 2002) motion estimation model offers a unified explanation for diverse motion illusions. In these cases, and in many others, the Bayesian model makes a substantial explanatory contribution that looks otherwise unachievable. The explanatory contribution includes *qualitative* predictions for disparate phenomenon coupled with *quantitative* predictions that closely match experimental data. From a scientific realist perspective, these explanatory achievements provide reason to believe that the model is approximately true.

The contrast with the pea plant study is glaring. Dener, Kacelnik, and Shemesh (2016) do not provide a Bayesian model of root growth. Indeed, they do not so much as hint which prior probability or prior likelihood such a model might include. They do not suggest, let alone argue, that a Bayesian model could offer a unified explanation for disparate phenomena or that it could yield quantitative predictions that closely match experimental data. There is not even a Bayesian model here that we can evaluate, much less a model that achieves anything approaching the explanatory success of the Bayesian dead reckoning model, the

Bayesian motion estimation model, or numerous other Bayesian cognitive science models. That is why Bayesian cognitive science supports the existence of credal states but the pea plant study, for all its interest, does not.

I agree with Block that a system can simulate (approximate) Bayesian inference. For example, a system might convert inputs into outputs by consulting a look-up table. More realistically, a system might acquire an input–output mapping through *reinforcement learning*. In reinforcement learning, the system receives rewards for how it responds to inputs, and it adjusts its responses to obtain optimal or near-optimal rewards. Systems trained through reinforcement learning can mimic certain kinds of approximate Bayesian inference (Weisswange et al., 2011). In principle, then, evolution might produce a system that operates *as if* it executes approximate Bayesian inference even though it does not actually execute approximate Bayesian inference. Nevertheless, I think it misleading to describe evolution as a "pro-instrumentalist mechanism." I see no reason why evolution should *favor* simulation of approximate Bayesian inference over implementation of approximate Bayesian inference.

When a scientific theory accurately predicts the behavior of a system, there is always a possibility that the theory is utterly false and that the system merely behaves *as if* the theory is true. For example, it is in principle possible that subatomic particles do not exist and that the physical universe merely behaves *as if* they exist. Physicists would only regard that in principle possibility as worth taking seriously if it were developed into a rival theory that matched modern physics in explanatory power. Similarly, we should only take seriously the suggestion that mental activity simulates rather than implements approximate Bayesian inference once it is developed into detailed models that rival current Bayesian models in explanatory power. So far, that has not happened. The scientific literature does not offer non-Bayesian models comparable in explanatory power to the Bayesian dead reckoning model, the Bayesian motion estimation model, or numerous other Bayesian models found in contemporary cognitive science. Perhaps impressive non-Bayesian models will eventually emerge. In their absence, the mere possibility that they might emerge should not worry realists about Bayesian cognitive science any more than the mere possibility of a successful physical theory that eschews subatomic particles should worry realists about subatomic particles.

5.3 The Argument From Altered Priors

I now rehearse an additional argument for realism regarding Bayesian cognitive science. My argument rests upon a crucial fact: input–output mappings rapidly change in response to changing environmental conditions. We have seen several examples:

- Shape and lightness perception change in response to stimuli that indicate a deviant lighting direction (Adams, Graf & Ernst, 2004).
- Motion perception changes in response to fast-moving stimuli (Sotiropoulos, Seitz & Seriès, 2011).
- The mapping from sensory inputs to motor commands changes in response to shifts in apparent finger position (Kording & Wolpert, 2004).
- Central tendency bias occurs in a wide range of domains, including perceptual estimation (Section 4.1) and dead reckoning (Section 4.3).

These experimental phenomena, and numerous others, conclusively demonstrate that the mapping from inputs to outputs is highly mutable.

Realists can easily explain in each case why the mapping changes as it does. They can say that the priors change so as to match changing environmental statistics. For example, suppose that a subject exhibits central tendency bias towards the mean of an experimentally imposed sample distribution, as in the (Petzschner & Glasauer, 2011) dead reckoning experiment. Realists explain the bias as follows: the prior shifts to match the sample distribution, which causes estimates to shift towards the mean of the distribution. Instrumentalists can acknowledge that the input–output mapping shifts, but they offer no principled explanation for *why* it shifts as it does. From an instrumentalist perspective, there is no principled reason why estimates should shift to match recent stimuli. The mere fact that a system simulates approximate Bayesian inference using certain priors provides no reason to expect that the system will change any particular way in response to changing environmental statistics. Hence, realism offers a major explanatory advantage over instrumentalism.

Call this *the argument from altered priors*. Although I have formulated the argument as applied to prior probabilities, similar argumentation applies to prior likelihoods and to posteriors (Rescorla, 2020c).

Block rejects the argument from altered priors: "I find this argument unconvincing because whatever it is about the computations of a system that simulates the effect of represented priors ... might also be able to simulate the effect of change of priors" (2018, p. 8).

I agree that, in principle, a system that simulates approximate Bayesian inference *given certain priors* might respond to changing environmental conditions by simulating approximate Bayesian inference *given another set of priors*. I question whether instrumentalists can develop that possibility into compelling models. The argument from altered priors is abductive: realism provides the best explanation for why input–output mappings change as they do. One does not undermine an abductive argument by noting that an alternative explanation may emerge. To undermine the argument from altered priors, one must provide a *specific* alternative explanation and show that it is at least as satisfying as the realist explanation.

In this connection, consider a system trained through reinforcement learning to simulate Bayesian inference *given certain priors*. By varying the rewards, we can train the system to simulate Bayesian inference *given another set of priors*. Accordingly, instrumentalists might hope that reinforcement learning can explain changes to the input–output mapping. In many cases, though, subjects receive either no feedback or extremely limited feedback on their performance. To illustrate, consider the (Petzschner & Glasauer, 2011) dead reckoning study. Participants received no feedback on their performance during each session, aside from a few initial training trials to ensure familiarity with the virtual reality setup. How, then, can reinforcement learning explain why subjects displayed central tendency bias? There was no "reward" to drive the ongoing change in learned responses. This study provides evidence that subjects iteratively update a distance prior in response to accumulated evidence.

Perhaps instrumentalist theories will eventually emerge that explain changing input–output mappings without an appeal to changing priors. We would then need to compare those instrumentalist theories with realist Bayesian theories. Until that time, we do well to develop the realist perspective and see where it leads.[11]

5.4 Neural Implementation

To gain more insight into the dialectic between realism and instrumentalism, let us consider the neural implementation of approximate Bayesian inference. How are credal states physically realized in the brain? Which neural operations implement computation of the (approximate) posterior from the priors? These questions do not arise for instrumentalists because instrumentalists do not regard credal states and transitions as psychologically real. For realists, the questions are pressing.

Computational neuroscientists have proposed several theories of how the brain might implement credal states and transitions (Fiser et al., 2010; Pouget et al., 2013; Rescorla, 2024). The proposed theories are biologically plausible and fit well with what we know about the brain, although no single theory has yet emerged as well-confirmed.

The credal states considered in Bayesian cognitive science are usually given by pdfs. Recall that a pdf determines probabilities assigned to intervals $[a, b]$.

---

[11] See Rescorla (2020c) for more on the argument from altered priors and for general defense of realism.

There are infinitely many of these intervals. The brain is a finite physical system and hence, as discussed in Section 3.4, cannot explicitly list each individual probability $P([a, b])$. Since the brain cannot enumerate the probability assigned to each interval, probabilities must be *implicitly* encoded by neural activity. The two main implicit encoding schemes under active consideration were mentioned in Section 3.4:

- *Parametric encoding*: the brain encodes parameters for the pdf. One possibility is that parameters are encoded by spike counts in a neural population (Ma et al., 2006). Each neuron is associated with a preferred stimulus value, and each neuron's spike count is interpreted as the strength of its "vote" for that stimulus value. "Votes" across the neural population determine parameters of a pdf, e.g., the mean and variance of a Gaussian. See Figures 35 and 36.
- *Sampling encoding*: the brain encodes a probability distribution via sampling propensities. For example, a neuron's membrane potential might encode a sample (Orbán et al., 2016). The objective chance distribution governing membrane potentials encodes the subjective probability distribution for the variable.

Computational neuroscientists have produced detailed neural network models that enshrine these encoding schemes. The models show how, in principle,

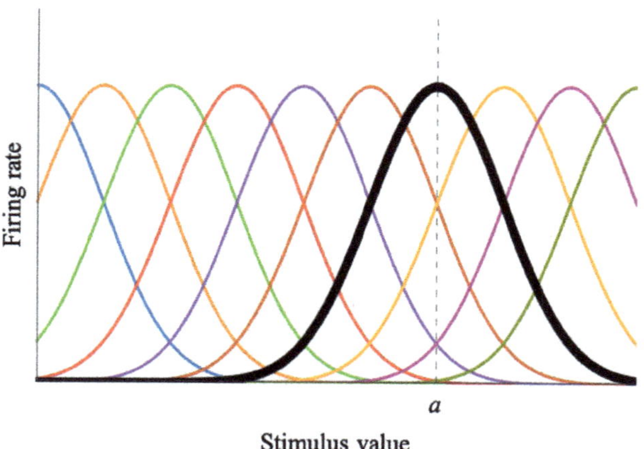

Figure 35 The *tuning curve* for a neuron summarizes the neuron's average response to a stimulus value. Figure 35 depicts tuning curves for a hypothetical neural population tuned to a one-dimensional continuous distal stimulus. The horizontal axis contains possible stimulus values. Each tuning curve depicts the average response (measured in spikes per second) of the corresponding neuron to possible stimulus values. Each tuning curve peaks at a preferred value of the stimulus. The black tuning curve has preferred stimulus value *a*.

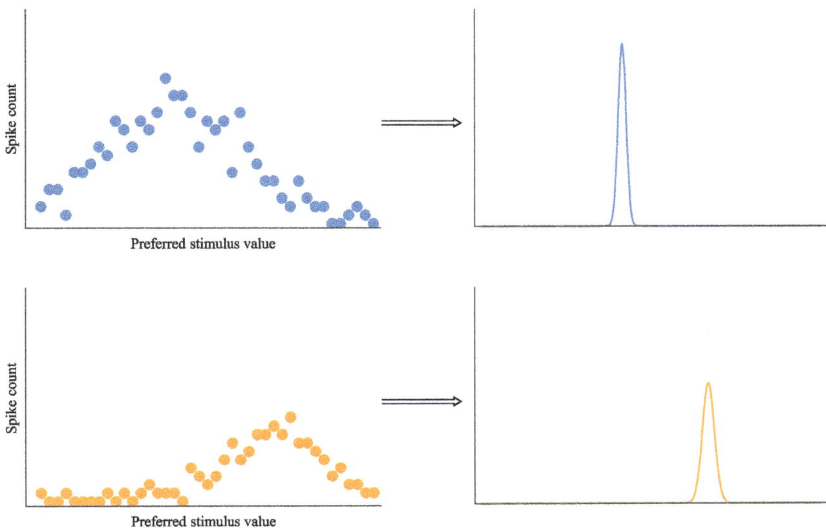

Figure 36 Heuristic illustration of how a neural population can implicitly encode parameters of a probability distribution. The top left panel depicts how a hypothetical neural population responds to a stimulus on a given occasion. The horizontal axis groups neurons according to preferred stimulus value. The vertical axis gives the spike count for each neuron during a fixed time interval. Spike counts encode a Gaussian distribution, depicted in the top right panel. The parametric encoding scheme used here is discussed in Beck et al. (2007): the mean of the Gaussian is a weighted average of stimulus values, where the weights are the individual spike counts; the variance is inversely proportional to the total spike count. The bottom left panel depicts a different neural response. The bottom right panel depicts the encoded Gaussian distribution, using the same encoding scheme.

a population of neurons could implement approximate Bayesian inference. Neuroscientists want to discover which implementation scheme(s) the brain actually uses.

Research into neural implementation of approximate Bayesian inference presupposes a broadly realist perspective on credal states and transitions (Ma, 2019; Rescorla, 2021a). If there are no priors, investigating how priors are realized in the brain is a waste of time. If the brain does not execute approximate Bayesian inference, investigating the neural operations that implement approximate Bayesian inference is a bad use of scientific resources. Thus, a major strand in current computational neuroscience presupposes a realist stance towards at least some Bayesian models.

Research into neural implementation also helps clarify realism's commitments. The core realist thesis is that priors and posteriors are genuine mental states that mediate between inputs and outputs. As genuine mental states, they must be neurally realized in some way or other. Realism is neutral about how exactly they are realized. In particular, realists do *not* claim that credal assignments are explicitly enumerated in the brain. On the contrary, realists recognize that explicit enumeration is impossible for most cases. They instead appeal to implicit encoding. They hold that credal states posited by Bayesian models are implicitly encoded by the brain. The implicit encoding scheme might be parametric, sampling, or something else entirely (e.g. Ganguli and Simoncelli, 2014). The brain may also use multiple encoding schemes simultaneously. Realism does not enshrine a commitment to any particular encoding scheme or class of encoding schemes.

6 Mental Representation

The previous section advanced a realist perspective on the credal states posited by Bayesian models. I now want to probe more deeply into the nature of the posited credal states. I will explore how they relate to the mind's *representational* nature.

The phrase "mental representation" is used many different ways in contemporary philosophy and psychology. My own usage reflects a tradition that traces back to Frege (1892/1997) and continues through contemporary figures such as Burge (2010) and Fodor (1975; 1987; 2008). According to this tradition, mental representation is connected with *veridicality-conditions*: conditions for veridically representing the world. Examples:

- Beliefs are the sorts of things that can be true or false. My belief *that Napoleon was born in Corsica* is true if Napoleon was born in Corsica, false if he was not.
- Intentions are the sorts of things that can be fulfilled or thwarted. My intention *to eat lentils for lunch* is fulfilled if I eat lentils for lunch, thwarted if I do not.
- Perceptual states are the sorts of things than can be accurate or inaccurate. Suppose I perceive object o as being a green cube. Then my perceptual state is accurate only if o is green and cubical.

Beliefs have truth-conditions, intentions have fulfillment-conditions, and perceptual states have accuracy conditions. Truth, fulfillment, and accuracy are species of veridicality.

Representational properties are properties that contribute or potentially contribute to veridicality-conditions. For example, suppose I have a belief about Napoleon. The mere fact that my belief is about Napoleon does not determine whether my belief is true or false. Nevertheless, my belief depends for its truth or falsity on how things are with Napoleon (rather than some other person). That my belief is about Napoleon helps determine the belief's truth-condition. So *being about Napoleon* is a representational property of my belief. Similarly, suppose I perceive some object as a green cube. The mere fact that my perceptual state represents green cubicality does not determine whether the state is accurate—accuracy also depends on *which* cube I am perceptually representing. Nevertheless, my perceptual state depends for its accuracy on whether the perceptually represented object is a green cube. That my perceptual state represents green cubicality helps determine the state's accuracy-condition. So *representing green cubicality* is a representational property of my perceptual state.

I will argue that credal states posited within Bayesian cognitive science have representational properties, and I will elucidate the explanatory role played by these representational properties.

6.1 Representational Explanation

Bayesian cognitive science seeks to explain mental and behavioral outcomes. It frequently characterizes the outcomes in representational terms. Examples:

- Perceptual psychology seeks to explain *illusions*. An illusion is a perceptual state that inaccurately represents the distal environment. So the science presupposes that perceptual states have accuracy-conditions.
- Sensorimotor psychology seeks to explain how the motor system chooses motor commands that promote the agent's goals. A goal may be fulfilled or thwarted. So the science presupposes mental states with fulfillment-conditions. These are *conative states*, i.e., mental states whose role is to initiate and sustain action. Often, the conative state is an *intention* (e.g. an intention to reach to a target). Burge (2022, pp. 502–530) argues that there also exist relatively low-level conative states lacking various features of intention, such as intention's characteristic ties to theoretical and practical reasoning, and that these low-level conative states set goals for motor control. For present purposes, the key point is that sensorimotor psychology presupposes goal-setting by mental states with fulfillment-conditions.
- Sensorimotor psychology seeks to explain why movement details vary more along *task-irrelevant* dimensions than *task-relevant* dimensions. The distinction between task-relevant and task-irrelevant dimensions presupposes a goal that may be fulfilled or thwarted.
- Research on human dead reckoning seeks to explain overshooting. To overshoot a location, the subject must have that location as a goal. So the science presupposes a conative mental state with a fulfillment-condition. Since human dead reckoning typically interfaces with fairly sophisticated planning

and decision-making, it seems likely that the conative state is typically an intention or something much like an intention. In some special cases, though, it may be a relatively low-level conative state more along the lines discussed by Burge.

As these examples illustrate, Bayesian cognitive science often characterizes explananda in representational terms.

The science also frequently characterizes explanantia, including credal states, in representational terms. Examples:

- The Bayesian dead reckoning model explains overshooting by positing a "slow speed" prior over self-motion. The prior causes the navigation system to underestimate displacement. To encode a prior that favors slow speeds, the navigation system must be able to represent speed. So the explanation of overshooting presupposes that the navigation system can represent speed. The explanation hinges upon a credal allocation over possible speeds, leading to an inaccurate displacement estimate.
- Bayesian perceptual psychology assumes that the perceptual system represents distal properties. It posits a prior regarding represented distal conditions (e.g. a prior that favors overhead lighting directions). When the prior is poorly calibrated to the perceiver's environment, the resulting perceptual estimates tend to be inaccurate. For example, the "light from overhead" prior produces inaccurate shape estimates in deviant conditions where light comes from below.
- To explain how the motor system promotes the agent's goals, Bayesian sensorimotor psychology posits sequential updating of credal assignments regarding the distal environment and the subject's own body. Credal assignments influence which motor commands are chosen. When credal assignments are poorly calibrated to the environment (e.g. the prior over shifts in finger position does not match actual finger shifts), the task goal tends to be thwarted.

Generally speaking, Bayesian cognitive science posits credal states regarding environmental conditions, including both distal properties (e.g. size, shape, color, location, density, etc.) and bodily properties (e.g. hand position). In describing credal states, researchers presuppose that the mind can represent the relevant environmental properties. Researchers characterize credal states by invoking representational relations to the environment. They cite these representationally-characterized credal states as explanantia.

Researchers in Bayesian cognitive science do not use the phrase "veridicality-condition." The speak instead of random variables, probability distributions, pdfs, and other entities drawn from probability theory. Nevertheless, their theorizing assigns a central role to veridicality-conditions. They identify both explananda and explanantia by citing representational properties: either veridicality-conditions or properties that potentially contribute to veridicality-conditions.

Take the Bayesian dead reckoning model. The model seeks to explain overshooting, which presupposes a conative state with a fulfillment-condition. To explain overshooting, the model posits that the navigation system underestimates displacement—in other words, that the displacement estimate is *inaccurate*. So the model explains overshooting by positing a mental state (the displacement estimate) that is evaluable as veridical or nonveridical. To explain why the navigation system underestimates displacement, the model posits a prior that favors slow speeds. The prior assigns credences to hypotheses regarding the creature's speed. For example, it assigns a credence to the hypothesis that the creature's speed lies in the interval $[a, b]$. This hypothesis is individuated through representational relations to possible speeds (namely, speeds lying between a and b). By citing credal assignments to representationally-individuated hypotheses, the model depicts the navigation system as favoring slow speeds. It thereby explains overshooting. Explanation is laced at every stage with appeals to representational properties.

Similarly, consider Bayesian modeling of size perception (Ernst & Banks, 2002; Helbig & Ernst, 2008). Here we posit a prior over possible distal sizes. The prior combines with sensory input (e.g. haptic or visual input) and a prior likelihood, yielding a posterior over possible distal sizes. On that basis, the perceptual system chooses a privileged size estimate, which goes into the final percept. The percept is veridical only if the perceived object has the estimated size. Thus, the final size estimate is individuated representationally—through its contribution to the percept's veridicality-condition. The prior and posterior are also characterized representationally. These are credal states that allocate credences over hypotheses regarding distal size. Hypotheses are individuated through their representational properties—through the distal sizes that they represent. So the model posits mental states with representational properties, mediating between proximal sensory input and the (representationally-characterized) perceptual size estimate.

One could offer a similar analysis for virtually every other explanation found within Bayesian cognitive science. Bayesian researchers frequently characterize explananda in representational terms. They almost invariably characterize credal states in representational terms. For that reason, their research fits well with the representationalist paradigm espoused by Burge (2010; 2022), Fodor (1975; 1987; 2008), Peacocke (1994; 1999), Pylyshyn (1984), Shea (2018), and many others.

6.2 Credal States Versus Mathematical Tools

I now develop my analysis by examining more closely the formal apparatus used by Bayesian modelers. The key point I wish to highlight is the distinction between *credal states* versus *the mathematical tools used to specify credal states*.

Look again at Figures 33 and 34. The green downward-sloping curve is a pdf: a function from $\mathbb{R}$ to $\mathbb{R}$. The pdf induces a probability distribution over sets of real numbers. The pdf and the induced probability distribution are mathematical tools that theorists use to specify the "slow speed" prior. The "slow speed" prior is a credal state: an assignment of credences to hypotheses. We must sharply distinguish the credal state from the pdf and also from the induced probability distribution. Nothing about the pdf *taken on its own* suggests we are modeling a credal state that concerns speed. The same pdf could just as well specify a prior over possible sizes, or possible distances, or any other one-dimensional continuous physical magnitude. The pdf in itself does not indicate that we are modeling a "slow speed" prior as opposed to a "small size" prior, a "short distance" prior, or numerous other possible priors. The same goes for the induced probability distribution.

Similar remarks apply to most other Bayesian models. The modeler typically specifies credal states through a probability distribution over sets of real numbers, which in turn is typically specified through a pdf. The probability distribution taken on its own does not even begin to dictate the underlying credal state. The credal state is defined over hypotheses that are individuated through their representational relations to the environment. The probability distribution is a mathematical function individuated without regard to any such representational relations. The same probability distribution could just as well specify many different credal states.

To identify the credal state specified by a pdf, we must look beyond mathematical formalism and consider the broader enterprise to which the formalism contributes. We must first ask which psychological domain is being modeled: perception, or motor control, or navigation, and so on. We must also ask which aspects of the environment are represented by the credal state: shape, or size, or color, or speed, and so on. Usually, we can answer these questions by studying the text that accompanies the formalism. For example, Lakshminarasimhan et al. (2018, p. 195) write that overshooting "can be explained by a model in which subjects maximized their expected reward under the influence of a slow-speed prior rather than by leaky integration of unbiased velocity estimates." This passage and kindred passages show that the pdf from Figures 33 and 34 is intended to specify a credal state that favors slow speeds and that is deployed during dead reckoning. Analogous passages abound throughout Bayesian cognitive science. These passages are not idle prattle or disposable heuristic. They play a crucial theoretical role: they point us towards the credal states specified by Bayesian models.

Pdfs are indispensable mathematical tools. They allow us to specify credal states with mathematical precision, and they allow us to bring the calculus of real numbers to bear. Ultimately, though, they omit something crucial. They omit the representational properties that help individuate credal states.

To bring the distinction between credal states versus mathematical tools into sharper relief, it helps to reflect upon *measurement units*. Using measurement units, we can describe a physical magnitude (such as a speed) with a real number. For example, we can say that an object's speed is 10 meters/sec. The physical magnitude is quite distinct from the number 10 that we use to measure it, as evidenced by the fact that a change in measurement units necessitates a change in the number used to specify the same physical magnitude. If we switch from meters/sec to feet/sec, we must now say that the object travels at

$$3.28084 \times 10 = 32.8084$$

feet/sec. We cite a different number to specify the same speed. Speeds are distinct from the numbers through which we measure speeds.[12]

When we specify a credal state through a pdf, our choice of pdf depends upon a canonical choice of measurement units. A change in measurement units necessitates a change in the pdf we use to specify the credal state. Figure 37 illustrates. The blue pdf corresponds to meters/sec. The orange pdf corresponds to feet/sec. The pdfs are different, but they specify the same underlying probability assignment over possible speeds. They specify the same "slow speed" prior. Full technical details are given in Section A5, but the point should be intuitively clear even absent any technical details. A pdf is defined over real numbers, so it can describe a credal allocation over possible speeds only relative to measurement units that map speeds to real numbers. If we change the measurement units, then we must use a different pdf to model the same credal allocation over speeds. The different pdf will induce a different probability distribution over sets of real numbers, even while the underlying credal allocation remains fixed.

Our choice of measurement units reflects our societal conventions, not inherent features of the credal state itself. There is no reason to suspect that pretheoretic human navigation employs our conventional measurement units.

---

[12] See Peacocke (2019) for a general account of physical magnitudes, including argumentation that we should add these items to our ontology.

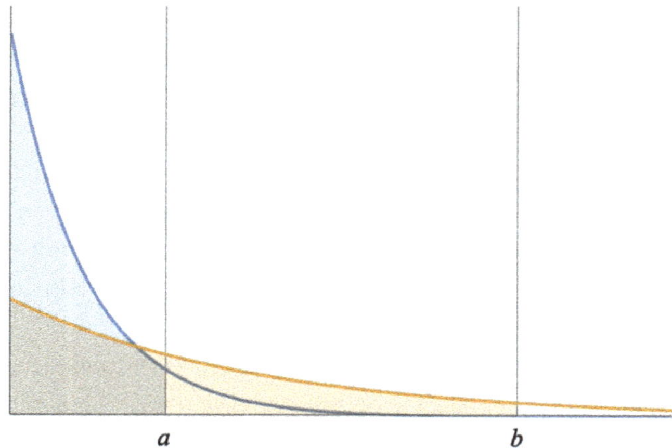

Figure 37 A change in measurement units necessitates a change in pdf. The blue pdf corresponds to meters/sec. The orange pdf corresponds to feet/sec. To convert from meters/sec to feet/sec, multiply by 3.28084. In Figure 37, $b = 3.28084 \times a$. The area under the blue curve over $[0, a]$ equals the area under the orange curve over $[0, b]$. The same equality holds for all other points a and b such that $b = 3.28084 \times a$. Thus, the two pdfs model the same probability assignment over possible speeds.

Indeed, it may not use any measurement units at all. (Cf. Peacocke, 2019, p. 48.) The same credal state could just as well be specified by a different pdf. For example, there is no reason to regard the blue pdf from Figure 37 as privileged over the orange pdf. Neither pdf has more psychological reality than the other. Psychological reality resides in the underlying credal state—a credal allocation over hypotheses regarding possible speeds—rather than the pdf.

The "slow speed" prior is a credal state that allocates credences over hypotheses, where the hypotheses are individuated through the specific speeds that they represent. The pdf is a purely mathematical function that reflects a conventional choice of measurement units. The prior does not reflect any such conventional choice. The pdf is a useful tool for specifying the underlying credal state, but its mathematical elegance should not dazzle us into ascribing psychological reality to it. The credal state is psychologically real. The pdf is not psychologically real, and neither is the induced probability distribution over sets of real numbers.

6.3 Random Variables Revisited

We can clarify the distinction between credal states and mathematical tools by revisiting the notion of *random variable*.

Recall from Section 2.3 that a random variable X maps an outcome space Ω to the real numbers $\mathbb{R}$. For example, suppose the outcome space Ω contains possible speeds of an asteroid. Each outcome ω in Ω is a speed that the asteroid might have. Speeds are physical magnitudes, not real numbers. Assuming a canonical choice of measurement units, we can measure magnitudes using real numbers. Let X be a random variable that maps each speed to the corresponding real number, using meters/sec as canonical units. Thus,

$$X(\omega) = x$$

when x specifies speed ω in meters/sec. X is a function from Ω (the set of possible speeds) to $\mathbb{R}$.

Given a random variable and an underlying outcome space Ω, we can use a probability distribution *over sets of real numbers* to specify a probability distribution *over sets of outcomes*. Continuing with the asteroid example, suppose we are given a probability distribution μ that assigns probabilities to sets of real numbers. Then we can use X and μ to assign probabilities *to sets of speeds*. For example, what probability should we assign to the event $X^{-1}[a, b]$? This event codifies the hypothesis *that the asteroid's speed falls between a and b*. If we are taking μ as a guide, we should assign the same probability to $X^{-1}[a, b]$ that μ assigns to $[a, b]$. In other words, if $P(X^{-1}[a, b])$ is the probability assigned to $X^{-1}[a, b]$, then we should have

$$P(X^{-1}[a, b]) = \mu([a, b]),$$

As Figure 38 illustrates, we can use X to transfer the probability distribution μ defined over *sets of real numbers* into a probability distribution P defined over

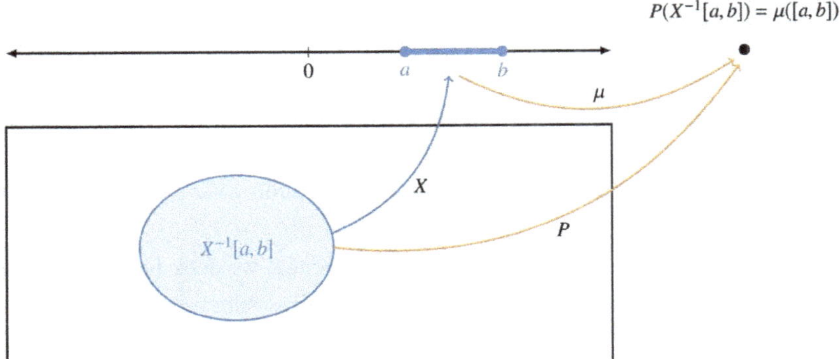

Figure 38 Illustrates the relation between P and μ. μ maps $[a, b]$ to the same probability as that to which P maps $X^{-1}[a, b]$.

sets of speeds. More generally, and as discussed more rigorously in Section A3, we can always use a random variable to transfer a probability distribution over sets of real numbers into a probability distribution over sets with members drawn from the underlying outcome space.

Now consider a different random variable Y that maps each magnitude to the corresponding real number using feet/sec. Thus,

$$Y(\omega) = y$$

when real number y specifies speed ω in feet/sec. Using the standard conversion from meters/sec to feet/sec, we obtain the following relation between X and Y:

$$Y(\omega) = 3.28084X(\omega).$$

The same magnitude ω is mapped to a different real number, depending on whether we are using meters/sec (corresponding to X) or feet/sec (corresponding to Y).

If we want to specify a fixed probability distribution P over sets whose members come from Ω itself, then X and Y mandate different probability distributions over sets of real numbers. Figure 37 illustrates. The pdf in blue generates one probability distribution over sets of real numbers. The pdf in orange generates a second probability distribution over sets of real numbers. Transferring the first probability distribution via X yields the same result as transferring the second probability distribution via Y. The very same probability distribution P over sets of speeds results if we use the blue pdf and X or if we use the orange pdf and Y.

These observations complement my diagnosis from Section 6.2. Our choice of pdf reflects our choice of a random variable, which reflects our choice of measurement units. Different measurement units mandate a different pdf in order to specify the same probability distribution over sets with members drawn from the underlying outcome space. These facts, which are basic to probability theory, reflect the inherently arbitrary nature of measurement using real numbers. Many different measurement units are equally legitimate. Different units yield different pdfs and different probability distributions over sets of real numbers, but the underlying probability distribution *over sets of outcomes* remains fixed.

In the special case of Bayesian cognitive science, we seek to model credal allocations by an agent or an agent's psychological subsystems (such as the perceptual system). The most convenient way to specify a credal allocation is usually through a pdf, as in Figures 33 and 34. The pdf is merely a tool for specifying a credal allocation over an underlying outcome space Ω. More precisely: the credal allocation assigns credences to sets whose members are drawn from Ω. The pdf depends upon an arbitrary choice of measurement units. The credal allocation does not. Psychological reality resides in the credal allocation, not the pdf.

6.4 The Objects of Credence

In Sections 6.2 and 6.3, I argued that the pdfs invoked by Bayesian cognitive scientists are mathematical tools for specifying credal states. A credal state assigns credences to sets of outcomes, where outcomes are drawn from an outcome space Ω. What are the outcomes? In other words, what are the elements of Ω? Answering this question is a large undertaking. I will broach a few preliminary considerations that should inform a more complete treatment.

Note first that Kolmogorov's axiomatization does not tell us what outcomes are. Kolmogorov assigns probabilities to *events*: sets whose members belong to an outcome space Ω. He places no constraints whatsoever upon Ω's members. Thus, the mathematical formalism of probability theory does not answer our question.

Explanatory practice within Bayesian cognitive science places some constraints upon Ω, but it does not dictate a unique answer. For example, the Bayesian dead reckoning model posits a prior over possible speeds, so outcomes must intimately relate *somehow* to speed. However, this constraint leaves room for various interpretations.

One interpretation is that Ω contains possible worlds. We would then construe events as sets of possible worlds. In the Bayesian dead reckoning model, the hypothesis *that the creature moves with speed between a and b* would be codified as *the set of possible worlds where the creature moves with speed between a and b*. In a Bayesian model of size perception, the hypothesis *that the perceived object has size between a and b* would be codified as *the set of possible worlds where the perceived object has size between a and b*. These codifications fit well with contemporary philosophical work, which often assigns credences to sets of possible worlds. More generally, they fit well with the longstanding philosophical tradition, mentioned in Section 2.1, of glossing propositions as sets of possible worlds.

A second interpretation is that Ω contains physical magnitudes. In the Bayesian dead reckoning model, the hypothesis *that the creature moves with speed between a and b* would be codified as *the set of speeds between a and b*. In a Bayesian model of size perception, the hypothesis *that the perceived object has size between a and b* would be codified as *the set of sizes between a and b*.

A third interpretation is that Ω contains *mental representations*. A mental representation is a mental item with representational properties. Mental representations are similar in key respects to the communal representations employed by human society, such as pictures, maps, or natural language sentences, but they are housed in the mind rather than the external world. They can be stored in memory, manipulated during mental activity, and combined to form complex representations. Appeal to mental representations is widespread in cognitive science theorizing (Carey, 2009; Fodor, 1975; Fodor, 2008; Gallistel & King, 2009; Pylyshyn, 1984; Rescorla, 2020d). If we take Ω to contain mental representations, then we will construe events as sets of mental representations. In the Bayesian dead reckoning model, the hypothesis *that the creature moves with speed between a and b* would be codified as something like *the set of mental representations that attribute speed between a and b*. In a Bayesian model of size perception, the hypothesis *that the perceived object has size between a and b* would be codified as something like *the set of mental representations that attribute size between a and b*. Although these codifications may look odd to philosophers reared on the possible worlds interpretation, they fit nicely with the widespread cognitive science commitment to mental representations.

Each of the three interpretations is compatible with a realist perspective on Bayesian cognitive science. Moreover, each interpretation codifies hypotheses in representational terms. The first interpretation collects together those possible worlds where the hypothesis is veridical. The second interpretation collects together those physical magnitudes that are consistent with the veridicality of the hypothesis. The third interpretation collects together mental representations according to which the hypothesis is veridical. Thus, all three interpretations analyze credal states representationally—in terms of veridicality-conditions or representational properties that contribute to veridicality-conditions.

All three interpretations deserve detailed consideration, as no doubt do other interpretations. My own sympathies lie with the third interpretation, but I will not attempt to defend it here. My goal instead is to highlight the need for *some* interpretation. To understand the credal states posited by Bayesian cognitive science, we must identify the entities to which credences attach. We must identify the objects of credence. Assuming that credences attach to sets, our task is to identify which elements belong to the sets. By making progress on this task, we may hope to illuminate the representational nature of credal states.[13]

---

[13] Mahtani (2024) conducts a detailed investigation into the objects of credence, focused primarily on the intersection of formal epistemology with philosophy of language rather than on Bayesian cognitive science.

6.5 How Many Outcomes?

In addition to studying what outcomes *are*, we must also consider *how many* outcomes there are. A set is *countable* when we can count its members using the numbers 0, 1, 2, 3, ... A set is *uncountable* when we cannot so count its members. A random variable is *discrete* when it has countably many possible values, *nondiscrete* when it has uncountably many possible values. The Bayesian dead reckoning model features a random variable whose possible values correspond to possible speeds of the navigator (specified through canonical measurement units). Even if we stipulate a maximum possible speed s, there are still uncountably many real numbers lying in the interval $[0, s]$ and hence uncountably many possible speeds. So the random variable is nondiscrete, and the underlying outcome space Ω is uncountable. Similarly for Bayesian modeling of motion estimation (Weiss, Simoncelli & Adelson, 2002), size estimation (Ernst & Banks, 2002), motor control (Todorov & Jordan, 2002), and numerous other tasks. In general, whenever cognitive scientists model Bayesian estimation of a physical magnitude that has uncountably many possible values (e.g. time, distance, speed, orientation, size), the resulting Bayesian model invokes a nondiscrete random variable X defined over an uncountable outcome space.

Taken literally, such a model attributes highly infinitary representational capacities. More specifically:

(i) The model posits credal states (a prior and a posterior) that assign probabilities to events $X^{-1}[a, b]$. There are uncountably many events $X^{-1}[a, b]$, so the model posits a credal assignment over uncountably many events.

(ii) The model posits credal states drawn from among uncountably many possible options. This remains so even if we demand that credal assignments belong to a fixed parametric family, such as the family of Gaussian distributions.

(iii) The model posits a privileged estimate x^* of X's value, as in Figure 28. There are uncountably many possible values x^*, so the model posits a privileged estimate selected from among uncountably many options.

Hence, the model attributes highly infinitary representational capacities when specifying both credal states and privileged estimates.

Some philosophers will bristle at these infinitary attributions. The attributions may look incompatible with obvious finitary limits on our representational or computational capacities. It might seem that we should dismiss (i)–(iii) as mere idealizations, eventually to be obviated by a more plausible model that honors the finitary limits on human mental activity. Shouldn't a plausible model restrict itself to a finite outcome space?

I agree that there are finitary limits *of some sort* on human representational and computational capacities. For example, we do not have infinite memory storage capacity: the mind cannot explicitly list infinitely many distinct pieces of information. Yet I wonder whether (i)–(iii) flout any genuine finitary limits on human mental activity. As discussed in Section 5.4, computational neuroscience offers various theories of how the brain could, in principle, implement or approximately implement Bayesian inference. The theories are biologically plausible, and they fit well with diverse neurophysiological data. Several theories describe the brain as implementing a Bayesian model that satisfies (i)–(iii). Those theories feature nondiscrete neural variables (e.g. membrane potential), which are taken to provide a substrate for credal states. Thus, (i)–(iii) look compatible with lots of work in contemporary computational neuroscience.

The classical computational theory of mind (CTM) holds that mental activity is digital computation (Fodor, 1975; 1987; 2008; Gallistel & King, 2009; Pylyshyn, 1984; Rescorla, 2020). A digital computing system has at most countably many possible computational states. Hence, CTM is incompatible with (ii) and (iii). However, CTM is compatible with (i). There is a well-developed framework—*computable probability theory*—that studies how digital computing systems can encode and compute over probability distributions (Ackerman, Freer & Roy, 2019). In this framework, the computing system often satisfies (i) but not (ii) or (iii). The system encodes a credal assignment over uncountably many events, but there are only countably many possible credal assignments and privileged estimates x^* available to the system. For example, the system may encode a Gaussian distribution, but there are only countably many distinct Gaussian distributions that it could have instead encoded (it can only encode a Gaussian whose mean and variance are drawn from a fixed countable set). In more practical terms, computer scientists and roboticists frequently program digital systems to compute over nondiscrete random variables (e.g. Thrun, Burgard & Fox, 2005). These systems encode a wide range of probability distributions, including Gaussian distributions and many others besides. Their computations satisfy (i) though not (ii) and (iii). Thus, proponents of CTM can happily allow that the mind assigns credences to uncountably many events.

Infinitary Bayesian models raise thorny questions at the intersection of philosophy, psychology, computation theory, and neuroscience.[14] I cannot hope to settle these questions here. For present purposes, the key point is that a realist representationalist perspective on Bayesian cognitive science admits several

---

[14] In particular, they engage longstanding debates over whether the mind executes *digital* versus *analog* computation. See Rescorla (2020a) for an introductory discussion.

divergent reactions to an explanatorily successful Bayesian model defined over a nondiscrete random variable, including the following three reactions:

- Accept the model at face value; embrace (i)–(iii).
- Guided by computable probability theory, emend the model by allowing only countably many of the credal states and estimates posited by the model; embrace (i) but not (ii) and (iii).
- Try to replace the model with a purely finitary approximation; reject (i)–(iii).

Each position is compatible with realism, which commits to credal states and transitions *approximately* like the ones posited by the model but does not insist that the model is literally true. Each position is compatible with representationalism, which champions the representational nature of credal states but does not mandate *infinitary* representational capacities.

7 Anti-representationalism

Anti-representationalists hold that we should expunge mental representation from rigorous scientific theorizing. They seek to explain mental and behavioral phenomena in strictly nonrepresentational terms. Different anti-representationalists favor different nonrepresentational paradigms:

- Quine (1960) favors Skinnerian *stimulus-response* psychology.
- Churchland (1981) favors a *neurophysiological* paradigm.
- Field (2001) and Stich (1983) favor *nonrepresentational computational description*.
- van Gelder (1992) favors *dynamical system theory*.

Despite these differences, anti-representationalists agree that mental representation makes no useful contribution to scientific theorizing about the mind.

Anti-representationalism conflicts with Bayesian cognitive science. As we have seen, Bayesian researchers routinely characterize explananda in representational terms. If we abjure representational discourse, then we cannot acknowledge those explananda. For example, anti-representationalists cannot replicate how the Bayesian dead reckoning model explains overshooting: overshooting is a representationally-characterized explanandum, because a subject can overshoot a location only when she has that location as a goal. Nor can anti-representationalists characterize a perceptual state as illusory: an illusion requires perceptual states with accuracy-conditions. Nonrepresentational theorizing ignores representational properties and hence cannot mention, let alone explain, representationally-characterized explananda. Since anti-representationalists cannot explain representationally-characterized explananda, they cannot replicate the explanatory benefits secured by Bayesian cognitive science.

Neither can anti-representationalists accept successful Bayesian explanations for *nonrepresentational* explananda. Suppose we characterize the results of dead reckoning in purely nonrepresentational terms. For example, we can identify the creature's final position across various trials, without mentioning whether the position overshoots any target location. The Bayesian dead reckoning model explains the nonrepresentationally characterized explanandum. It does so by isolating causally relevant factors (including the "slow speed" prior) that influence position. This is a representational explanation: it explains a nonrepresentational explanandum (position) by citing a credal allocation over representationally-characterized hypotheses. Anti-representationalists cannot accept the explanation. Their anti-representationalist scruples forbid explanations that cite representational properties of mental states.

Anti-representationalists claim that we can replicate any purported benefits of representational explanation through alternative explanations couched in purely nonrepresentational terms. They claim that we can jettison mental representation while preserving the explanatory achievements enabled by representationally-characterized explanantia. The long, dismal history of anti-representationalist theorizing provides little basis for that claim. Anti-representationalists have consistently failed to match even the most elementary explanatory achievements of representationalist cognitive science. For example, Gibson's (1979) *direct perception* framework seeks to analyze perception in nonrepresentational terms, but it cannot explain a huge range of perceptual illusions and constancies (Fodor & Pylyshyn, 1981). Similar remarks apply to numerous other anti-representationalist theories that have flitted in and out of fashion over the past century.

In the present dialectical context, the key question is whether anti-representationalists can preserve the explanatory benefits of Bayesian models without invoking representational mental states. I doubt it. One cannot usually strip a scientific theory of its main theoretical concepts while retaining its explanatory benefits. For example, renouncing talk about subatomic particles would severely limit the explanatory power of physics. I see no reason to think that we can renounce talk about representational credal states while retaining the explanatory benefits provided by such talk. Consider the Bayesian dead reckoning model. It relies in an essential way upon the "slow speed" prior. By invoking this prior, the model achieves a much better fit with experimental data than the hitherto dominant "leaky integrator" model. The "slow speed" prior is characterized in representational terms. How, then, can we replicate its explanatory contribution while eschewing representational discourse? The principal explanatory advance made by the model was a posit of representational mental states.

To support my viewpoint, I will now critique two anti-representationalist interpretations of Bayesian cognitive science. The interpretations differ in various ways. They agree that, contrary to what I suggested in Section 6, Bayesian models of the mind do *not* postulate representational mental states. I will explain why I think both interpretations are mistaken.

7.1 Function-theoretic Computation

Egan (2010; 2020) advocates a *function-theoretic* approach to mental computation: "The input of a computationally characterized mechanism represents the arguments and the outputs the values of a mathematical function that canonically specifies the task executed by the mechanism" (2020, p. 33, fn. 7). A computational theory of a mechanism "comprises a specification of the function (in the mathematical sense) computed by the mechanism" (2020, p. 33). Thus, computational psychology provides "an abstract mathematical description" that prescinds from representational properties of mental states (Egan, 2010, p. 256). She admits that cognitive scientists frequently mention representational properties when describing mental states. She maintains that representational discourse "is best construed as a kind of gloss—an *intentional* gloss—on the computational theory" (2020, p. 33). The intentional gloss plays a useful heuristic role in our theorizing: it helps us connect our computational description with representationally-characterized explananda; it helps us track how the computational mechanism responds to environmental events; and it can serve as a temporary placeholder until we discover an underlying computational mechanism. Representational properties do not figure in genuinely computational theories and are not necessary for good cognitive science explanations: "the computational theory proper can fully explain the interaction between organism and environment . . . without adverting to cognitive content" (2020, p. 34).

Egan's function-theoretic approach encompasses the following three doctrines, each of which I reject:

(a) Computational models of the mind mention inputs and outputs, but they do not mention internal states that mediate between inputs and outputs.

(b) Computational models describe inputs and outputs in purely mathematical terms, without mentioning any representational properties of the inputs or outputs.

(c) Representational discourse plays a purely heuristic role in cognitive science theorizing. It makes no genuine explanatory contribution.

I will critique doctrines (a)–(c) in turn.

Doctrine (a) conflicts with huge amounts of cognitive science theorizing. Computational modeling by cognitive scientists routinely posits internal states that mediate between inputs and outputs. All the Bayesian models I have discussed above are examples. For example, Bayesian models of perception as encapsulated by Figure 28 posit three internal credal states: a prior probability, a prior likelihood, and a posterior (or approximate posterior). These credal states mediate between the input (proximal sensory stimulation) and the output (a privileged perceptual estimate of a distal property). More complex models, such as models of motor control, posit a *sequence* of credal states mediating between inputs and outputs. Evidently, Bayesian models commit to far more internal computational detail than (a) allows. The models do not merely describe a function from inputs to outputs. They say something informative about the internal states and transitions through which the system converts inputs into outputs.

Egan disagrees. She asserts that Bayesian models carry "no commitment to internal states or structures and causal processes defined on them" (2020, p. 48) and that "Bayesian models, to the extent that they say anything about how the brain actually works, give ... a *function-theoretic* characterization; they specify the function, in the mathematical sense, computed by the mechanism" (2020, p. 50). She does not justify her analysis by adducing a single Bayesian model found in cognitive science. She does not attempt to reconcile her analysis with the commitment, apparently ubiquitous throughout Bayesian cognitive science, to credal states and transitions. She simply states, without evidence or argument, that Bayesian models are not committed to any internal states or processes.

Egan professes neutrality in the debate between realist versus instrumentalist perspectives on Bayesian modeling (2020, p. 49, fn. 22). Yet her analysis seems irreconcilable with the most faintly realist perspective. On anything resembling realism, we should accept the existence of credal states and transitions mediating between inputs and outputs. Only if we adopt a strongly instrumentalist perspective may we regard a Bayesian model as specifying a mere function from inputs to outputs. I indicated in Section 5 why I favor realism over instrumentalism.

Doctrine (b) is also problematic, at least as applied to Bayesian modeling of the mind. Bayesian models routinely specify either inputs or outputs in representational terms:

- Bayesian sensorimotor models specify a task goal as input to sensorimotor processing. The goal is set by a conative state with a fulfillment-condition. Hence, the Bayesian model presupposes a representationally-specified mental state.

- Bayesian perceptual models usually yield as output a perceptual estimate of some distal property. Estimates can be accurate or inaccurate. An estimate that an object has a certain size is accurate only if the object has that size; an estimate that an object moves with a certain speed is accurate only if the object moves with that speed; and so on.

These representational descriptions are inherent to the computational model. They are all we have to go on when identifying the relevant inputs or outputs. For example, suppose a Bayesian model outputs an estimate of an object's size. The model individuates the estimate through its representational relation to a specific distal size. If we abandon any reference to represented size, we abandon our only way of identifying the model's outputs.

Doctrine (c) is similarly problematic. As I documented in Section 6, Bayesian models routinely individuate credal states in representational terms. Abandoning representational discourse leaves us with no way to identify the credal states postulated by the model and hence no way to replicate an explanation that cites those credal states. For example, suppose a Bayesian perceptual model posits a prior over distal size. If we refuse to mention sizes represented by the perceptual system, then we cannot identify the hypotheses to which the prior assigns credences, so we cannot cite the prior to explain anything. Accordingly, I disagree with Egan's claim that "Bayesian models are typically not developed at a level of description that allows us to assess their representational commitments, in the relevant sense. They have no representational commitments, in the relevant sense" (2020, p. 48). Once again, Egan does not provide any concrete examples to validate her assessment. She does not indicate, for even a single case, how we are to individuate credal states in nonrepresentational terms. The lack of detail is not surprising, since a nonrepresentational individuative scheme looks fundamentally incompatible with the core methodology of Bayesian cognitive science.

Egan is certainly correct that Bayesian cognitive science uses mathematical tools to characterize inputs, outputs, and mediating credal states. Inputs and outputs are typically described using real numbers. Mediating credal states are usually described using pdfs. So Bayesian modeling includes "abstract mathematical descriptions" somewhat along the lines favored by Egan. As explained in Sections 6.2 and 6.3, these mathematical descriptions reflect our arbitrary, conventional choice of measurement units. Psychological reality and explanatory power reside in the representational states specified by our mathematical descriptions, not in the mathematical descriptions themselves. For example, if we describe the perceptual system as estimating that an object has size s, the specific real number s reflects our arbitrary choice of units for measuring size.

The number has no psychological reality. It explains nothing. What is psychologically real is that the perceptual estimate represents a specific size—a physical magnitude, not a real number. Similarly, if we describe a credal state using a pdf, the pdf reflects our arbitrary choice of measurement units. It has no psychological reality. It explains nothing. The credal state is what does the explaining.

The mathematical descriptions emphasized by Egan are artifacts of our measurement conventions. Different measurement units would yield a different mathematical description, including a different function from inputs to outputs, while leaving representational description the same. Representational description, not mathematical description, is the locus of psychological reality and explanatory power. For example, suppose we learn that a Bayesian dead reckoner estimates speed 5. Does that knowledge in itself help us explain overshooting? No. We need to specify measurement units! 5 meters/sec, or 5 feet/sec, or something else? The number 5 by itself is explanatorily irrelevant. What matters is the physical magnitude measured by 5—that is, the speed represented by the dead reckoner. The represented magnitude, not the number, is explanatorily important. Similar remarks apply to other mathematical descriptions found in Bayesian cognitive science, including specification of pdfs.

I critiqued Egan along these lines in previous work (Rescorla, 2015a). Egan deems my critique "very puzzling" (2020, p. 48) and retorts (2020, p. 50):

> To think that commitment to Bayes' theorem—a function defined on probability distributions—reflects an arbitrary choice of conventions is analogous to thinking that a claim that a device computes the addition function reflects a commitment to represent addends and sums in base 10. Contra Rescorla, to the extent that Bayesian models are to be construed realistically … such proposals should be construed as hypotheses about underlying psychological reality, committed, in particular, to the claim that the system is computing an approximation to Bayes' theorem.

I respond as follows:

- Bayes's theorem is not "a function defined on probability distributions." It is a theorem.
- I agree with Egan that "commitment to Bayes's theorem" does not "reflect an arbitrary choice of conventions." Bayes's theorem does not in any way depend for its truth upon our conventions.
- As a realist about Bayesian cognitive science, I do indeed hold that the mind often computes an approximation to the posterior. I hold that at least some Bayesian models describe mental processes with at least approximate accuracy.

- When we describe a device as computing the addition function, we are not committed to using base 10 notation. Nor are we committed to saying that *the device* uses base 10 notation. There are many possible numerical notations that a device might use to compute arithmetical functions.
- When we describe a credal state using a pdf, our choice of pdf reflects our arbitrary measurement units for the represented environmental variable. Our description does not commit us to saying that the mind uses those particular measurement units. For example, it is highly unlikely that the human navigation system measures speed using meters/sec.
- Egan claims that abstract mathematical description of mental computation has explanatory priority over representational description. This position is implausible because the mathematical description typically reflects an arbitrary choice of measurement units.

My conclusion: Egan's response gives no reason to attribute any psychological reality to abstract mathematical descriptions or to question the explanatory centrality that I attribute to representational descriptions.

In summary, Egan's function-theoretic conception does not fit well with Bayesian cognitive science because it neglects the crucial role that Bayesian modeling assigns to representational descriptions of explananda and explanantia. In place of representational descriptions, Egan commends abstract mathematical descriptions. Yet abstract mathematical descriptions reflect our own arbitrary measurement units and lack any psychological reality. Egan's nonrepresentational approach cannot preserve the most basic explanatory achievements of Bayesian cognitive science.

7.2 Radical Enactivism

Hutto and Myin (2017) espouse a *radical enactivist* approach to cognitive science. They view cognition as a dynamic interaction between an embodied brain and a changing environment. They "conceive of the basis of cognition in terms of extensive and dynamically loopy processes that are responsive to information in the form of environmental variables spanning multiple spatial and temporal scales" (p. 9). They also reject representationalism: they "construe cognition as unfolding, world-relating processes rather than as a series of content-bearing states and their interactions" (p. 9). They acknowledge that talk about veridicality-conditions is illuminating when applied to sophisticated symbolic communication (p. 90). They deny that it usefully contributes to theorizing about perception, motor control, or other relatively low-level psychological domains (pp. 12–13).

Hutto and Myin apply their radical enactivist approach to Bayesian cognitive science. Following Clark (2015) and Hohwy (2014), they focus almost exclusively upon a neural implementation framework called *predictive coding*. The basic idea behind predictive coding is that the brain generates a prediction regarding the sensory input it will receive. The brain compares its prediction with actual sensory input, computing a *prediction error* term. Prediction error informs subsequent computation, shaping future expectations so as to minimize future prediction error. Many predictive coding models have a hierarchical structure: higher levels of the network compute predictions about lower-level activity, and the lower level computes a prediction error term that is transmitted back to the higher level. There is nothing inherently Bayesian about predictive coding models, but when set up in the right way they can implement an approximation to Bayesian inference. This can be done either through parametric encoding (Friston, 2010) or through sampling encoding (Lee & Mumford, 2003). Hutto and Myin use the label *the Predictive Processing account of Cognition* (PPC) to describe theories that implement approximate Bayesian inference through predictive coding.

Hutto and Myin offer a radical enactivist interpretation of PPC. Their core interpretive claim is that we need not gloss talk about "prediction" and "expectation" in representational terms. They write: "Having expectations about what we will experience sensorily need not be thought of as involving the making of any kind of contentful claim about the state of the world. Nor need we think of sensory perturbations that are involved in such matches and mismatches as supplying rich contentful messages that contradict the content of our expectation" (pp. 70–71). Accordingly, we need not interpret PPC models representationally: "our expectations can fail to match incoming sensory experience without this activity being construed as a content-based operation" (p. 71). They conclude that PPC provides no support for representationalism.

I agree with Hutto and Myin that, in many cases, we should not interpret PPC talk about "prediction" and "expectation" in representational terms. I agree that, in many cases, we should not describe the mind as "representing" expected experiences. As Burge (2010, pp. 367–463) notes, there is no evidence that the perceptual system represents proximal sensory stimulations. The perceptual system converts nonrepresentational sensory stimulations into perceptual representations, without representing the stimulations. There is no explanatory benefit to saying that the perceptual system represents its own sensory input. When a PPC neural network compares predicted sensory input with actual sensory input, we usually should not describe the comparison in representational terms. We should instead say that the network compares an input signal with a feedback signal generated by a higher level of the network. We may describe both signals in neural terms, e.g., as firing rates, and we may describe the "prediction error" computation as a neurophysiological operation on those signals. Representational properties play no role in characterizing the "prediction error" computation.

A similar diagnosis applies to higher levels in hierarchical PPC models, such as the celebrated (Rao & Ballard, 1999) model. Each level compares neural activity with a feedback "prediction" signal received from a higher level, computing an "error" term subsequently transmitted to the higher level. The feedback signal and the "error" computation can again be described in non-representational, neurophysiological terms.

Typically, then, we should not describe a PPC neural network as representing its inputs or its own neural activity. The network *receives but does represent* proximal sensory inputs. It *instantiates but does not represent* neural activity. Talk about "prediction" and "expectation" may be harmless enough for some purposes, but I agree with Hutto and Myin that we achieve no explanatory gain by glossing this talk in representational terms.[15]

However, the nonrepresentational interpretation of prediction talk is doubly irrelevant to representationalism about Bayesian cognitive science.

First, we should not focus exclusively on PPC models. Most Bayesian modeling is not tied to the PPC research program. Most Bayesian models found in cognitive science are neutral about neural implementation mechanisms. Many promising implementation schemes, such as the schemes discussed in Ma et al. (2006) and Orbán et al. (2016), do not feature anything like predictive coding (Rescorla, 2017; Rescorla, 2024). Thus, the interpretation of PPC modeling is distinct from the interpretation of Bayesian modeling more generally. Hutto and Myin give no reason for focusing narrowly on PPC to the exclusion of generic Bayesian modeling. Indeed, their exposition tends to elide the difference between PPC and Bayesian cognitive science (e.g. pp. 150–151). Although predictive coding has received considerable recent attention in the philosophical community, empirical support for it remains equivocal (Aitchison & Lengyel, 2017). In my opinion, we currently have no reason to suspect that approximate Bayesian inference is typically implemented in PPC fashion.

Second, and more importantly, representationalists about Bayesian cognitive science do not claim that the mind represents either sensory input or neural activity. Representationalists claim that the mind represents *environmental* conditions, including both distal conditions and bodily state. Assume for the sake of argument that a neural system implements approximate Bayesian inference through a predictive coding implementation mechanism. We will describe the system using a Bayesian model, which posits credal states and

---

[15] See also Cao (2020) for critical discussion of talk about "prediction" in the context of predictive coding models. See Burge (2022, pp. 631–632) for more general cautionary remarks regarding talk about "prediction" and "expectation" in psychological theorizing.

transitions, and a PPC model, which specifies how the Bayesian model is neurally implemented by a predictive coding mechanism. I agree with Hutto and Myin that there is no reason to think that the system represents its own inputs or own neural activity. Nevertheless, we have strong reason to think that the system represents *the environment*. We have strong reason to describe the system's credal states in representational terms, as allocating credences over representationally-individuated hypotheses. Only then can we preserve explanations that rely on representationally-characterized credal states. For example, how can we explain overshooting in dead reckoning unless we posit a prior that favors slower speeds? I have no idea how enactivists would interpret the "slow speed" prior in nonrepresentational terms, let alone how the ensuing explanations would work.

Hutto and Myin (pp. 151–155) express skepticism about my representationalist interpretation of Bayesian models. They do not provide a developed alternative interpretation. They do not indicate how to gloss credal states and transitions in nonrepresentationalist enactivist terms. In fact, they barely discuss credal states: they mention priors a mere handful of times, and they do not mention posteriors at all. They do not analyze a single specific Bayesian model of mental activity, even in the most schematic way. Their treatment gives no hint how enactivists might eschew representational vocabulary while preserving the explanatory power of Bayesian modeling.

7.3 Interpreting Bayesian Cognitive Science

When philosophers interpret a scientific theory, they often employ theoretical notions (such as *veridicality-condition*) that play no explicit role in scientific discourse. Inevitably, there is a gap between philosophical interpretation and scientific texts. Still, some interpretations usually fit much better with scientific practice than others.

In the present case, a representationalist interpretation fits much better with Bayesian cognitive science than the function-theoretic interpretation offered by Egan or the enactivist interpretation offered by Hutto and Myin. The representationalist interpretation describes how to interpret the priors and posteriors that figure so prominently in Bayesian theorizing. The function-theoretic and enactivist conceptions say virtually nothing about how to interpret priors and posteriors, save perhaps to dismiss them in instrumentalist fashion as useful fictions. The representationalist interpretation analyzes in quite precise detail the explanations offered by Bayesian cognitive scientists, such as the explanations embodied by Figures 33 and 34. The function-theoretic and enactivist interpretations have little if anything to say about those explanations. Absent more compelling anti-representationalist interpretations, the representationalist interpretation looks secure.

8 Conclusion

The mind operates amid constant uncertainty stemming from multiple sources, including noise, ambiguous input, and conflicting sensory cues. Bayesian cognitive science postulates that the mind grapples with uncertainty by implicitly encoding credal assignments over hypotheses. The encoded credences influence inference and decision-making, roughly in accord with Bayesian norms. The Bayesian program draws support from strong empirical evidence across a range of psychological domains.

I have analyzed Bayesian modeling from a realist representationalist perspective that takes seriously the postulation of credal states and transitions. Realists hold that, when a Bayesian model is explanatorily successful, we have good reason to accept the existence of credal states and transitions roughly like those posited by the model. Representationalists hold that the posited credal states assign credences to hypotheses individuated through their representational properties. The realist representationalist interpretation fits much better with scientific practice than do rival instrumentalist or anti-representationalist interpretations.

Throughout my discussion, I have highlighted foundational questions raised by the Bayesian paradigm. Which mental processes approximately conform to Bayesian norms, and which do not? How do nature and nurture jointly influence priors employed by the mind? How are credal states neurally implemented? How does the brain transition from one credal state to another? What computational strategies does it use to approximate intractable Bayesian inferences? What is it to attach a credence to a hypothesis? Given that hypotheses are sets of outcomes, what exactly are the outcomes? How literally should we construe an infinitary Bayesian model built atop an uncountable outcome space? Ongoing research into these and other foundational questions promises to illuminate how the representational mind, by approximating rational norms, copes with perpetual uncertainty.

Appendix: Foundations of Probability Theory

This appendix presents some key probabilistic concepts as they relate to Bayesian modeling. It serves as a more mathematically rigorous complement to the informal exposition from Sections 2 and 3.

A few preliminary definitions are in order. Let A and B be sets. A function f from A to B is an *injection* iff $f(a)$ and $f(b)$ are distinct whenever a and b are distinct. A function f from A to B is a *surjection* iff, for each $b \in B$, there exists $a \in A$ such that $f(a) = b$. A *bijection* is a function that is an injection and a surjection. $\mathbb{N}$ is the set of *natural numbers*: $\{0,\ 1,\ 2,\ 3, \ldots\}$. A is *infinite* iff there exists an injection from $\mathbb{N}$ to A. A is *countably infinite* iff there exists a bijection from $\mathbb{N}$ to A. A is *countable* iff it is finite or countably infinite. A is *uncountable* iff it is infinite but not countably infinite. $\mathbb{R}$ is the set of real numbers. $[a, b]$ is $\{x \in \mathbb{R} : a \le x \le b\}$. $\mathbb{R}^n$ is the set of n-tuples drawn from $\mathbb{R}$, that is,

$$\{(x_1, x_2, \ldots, x_n): x_i \in \mathbb{R},\ \textit{for all}\ i\}.$$

Recall that $\mathbb{R}$ is uncountable, as is $\mathbb{R}^n$, and that $[a, b]$ is uncountable whenever $a \neq b$.

A1 Measurable Spaces

In Kolmogorov's axiomatization, probabilities attach to sets whose members are drawn from an outcome space Ω. The *powerset* of Ω is the set containing all subsets of Ω. We notate it as $\mathcal{P}(\Omega)$. When Ω is finite, we can assign probabilities to all members of $\mathcal{P}(\Omega)$. When Ω is uncountable, it is often impossible to assign intuitively plausible probabilities to all members of the powerset (Proschan & Shaw, 2016, pp. 17–35). Instead, probability theorists assign probabilities to certain *privileged* members of $\mathcal{P}(\Omega)$. The privileged members, called *events*, form a *σ-field over* Ω. A σ-field over Ω is a subset $\mathcal{F}$ of $\mathcal{P}(\Omega)$ such that:

Ω belongs to $\mathcal{F}$.

If H belongs to $\mathcal{F}$, then H^c belongs to $\mathcal{F}$.

If $H_1, H_2, \ldots, H_n, \ldots$ belong to $\mathcal{F}$, then their union $\bigcup_n H_n$ also belongs to $\mathcal{F}$.

The union $\bigcup_n H_n$ is the set containing all elements that belong to at least one of the sets H_n. There may be a countable infinity of sets H_n.

We typically choose a σ-field that arises organically from our interests. For example, suppose we are modeling an asteroid's speed using outcome space $\mathbb{R}$.

A natural question is whether the asteroid's speed x falls in the interval $[a, b]$. We would like to assign probabilities to all these intervals. At the very least, then, our σ-field should contain every interval $[a, b]$. Consider the *minimal* σ-field containing all intervals $[a, b]$. Call it $\mathcal{B}$. Intuitively: we throw just enough sets into $\mathcal{B}$ to ensure that $\mathcal{B}$ contains each interval $[a, b]$ and is closed under complementation and countable union. $\mathcal{B}$'s members are called the *Borel* sets. $\mathcal{B}$ usually serves as the most natural σ-field when the outcome space is $\mathbb{R}$. Similarly, suppose that the outcome space is $\mathbb{R}^2$, i.e., the set of ordered pairs of real numbers. Consider the minimal σ-field containing all *rectangles*. Elements of this σ-field are again called Borel sets. The same construction generalizes to $\mathbb{R}^n$, for arbitrary n.

An outcome space Ω along with a σ-field $\mathcal{F}$ form a *measurable space*, typically notated as $(\Omega, \mathcal{F})$.

A2 Probability Measures

We now consider a function P that assigns probabilities to events belonging to $\mathcal{F}$. For each $H \in \mathcal{F}$, $P(H)$ is the probability assigned to H. As indicated in Section 2.2, Kolmogorov places three axiomatic constraints on P. Here are the first two axioms:

$$0 \leq P(H) \leq 1.$$

$$P(\Omega) = 1.$$

As for the third axiom (additivity), recall my formulation from Section 2.2:

$$P(H_1 \cup H_2) = P(H_1) + P(H_2)$$

when H_1 and H_2 are disjoint. This formulation is called *finite additivity*. Assuming finite additivity, one can easily prove:

$$P(H_1 \cup H_2 \cup \ldots \cup H_n) = P(H_1) + P(H_2) + \ldots + P(H_n) \tag{5}$$

when $H_1, H_2, \ldots, H_n$ is a finite list of pairwise disjoint events. See Figure 39. Kolmogorov assumes a stronger axiomatic constraint that generalizes (5) to a potentially infinite list of pairwise disjoint events $H_1, H_2, \ldots, H_n, \ldots$ The stronger constraint, called *countable additivity*, demands that:

$$P\left(\bigcup_n H_n\right) = \sum_n P(H_n),$$

where $\bigcup_n H_n$ is the countable union of the H_n. Kolmogorov's axiomatization employs countable additivity as opposed to mere finite additivity.

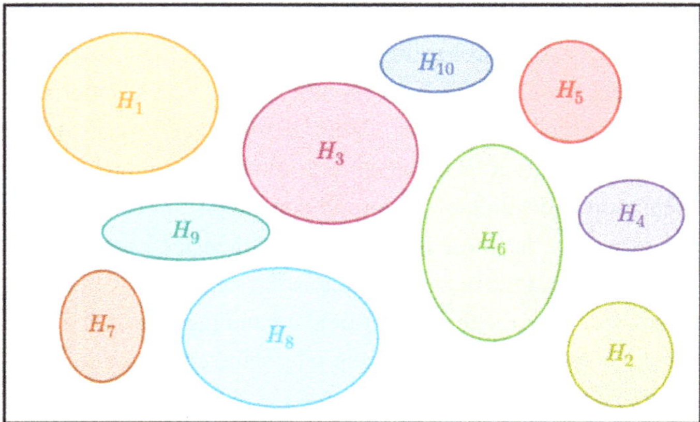

Figure 39 H_1, H_2, ..., H_{10} are pairwise disjoint events. Finite additivity requires that their union (the total shaded area) receive a probability equal to the sums of the probabilities assigned to them individually.

Countable additivity offers an important advantage over mere finite additivity: it constrains the probabilities assigned to many more events. Using countable additivity, we can extrapolate probability assignments from elementary events (e.g. intervals of real numbers) to numerous complex events left unaddressed by mere finite additivity (e.g. countable unions of disjoint intervals). Accordingly, countable additivity is widely assumed within probability theory (Billingsley, 1995). Some versions of Bayesian decision theory employ only finite additivity (e.g. de Finetti, 1972; Savage, 1972), but most versions assume countable additivity (e.g. DeGroot, 1970; Easwaran, 2013; Ghosal & van der Vaart, 2017; Gelman et al., 2014). In a Bayesian context, the dispute between finite and countable additivity is a normative one. It concerns the norms governing rational allocation of credence over a hypothesis space. Proponents of countable additivity claim that rational credences should be countably additive, while opponents maintain that rational credences need only be finitely additive. For discussion of finite versus countable additivity in the Bayesian context, see Liu (2020).

When a probability assignment P satisfies all three axioms (including countable additivity), it is called a *probability measure* (or a *probability distribution*), and $(\Omega, \mathcal{F}, P)$ is called a *probability space*.

A3 Random Variables Defined Rigorously

Let X be a function from Ω to $\mathbb{R}$. To assign probabilities to hypotheses regarding X's possible values, we must ensure that our σ-field $\mathcal{F}$ contains all the hypotheses. For each $B \in \mathcal{B}$, let

$$X^{-1}(B) =_{df} \{\omega \in \Omega : X(\omega) \in B\}.$$

X is a *random variable* on the probability space $(\Omega, \mathcal{F}, P)$ iff

$$X^{-1}(B) \in \mathcal{F}, \text{ for every } B \in \mathcal{B}.$$

This condition ensures that, for each Borel set B, $\mathcal{F}$ contains the hypothesis that X's value falls within B. For example, $\mathcal{F}$ includes each event $X^{-1}[a, b]$. For any real number x, the event

$$\{\omega \in \Omega : X(\omega) = x\}$$

is typically notated as

$$X = x.$$

We may write $P(X = x)$ for the probability that X has value x (e.g. the probability that the asteroid has speed x). Similarly, the event

$$\{\omega \in \Omega : X(\omega) \neq x\}$$

is typically notated as

$$X \neq x.$$

We may write $P(X \neq x)$ for the probability that X does not have value x.

Given a probability space $(\Omega, \mathcal{F}, P)$ and a random variable X, we can define a probability measure μ over the measurable space $(\mathbb{R}, \mathcal{B})$:

$$\mu(B) =_{df} P\left(X^{-1}(B)\right), \text{for every } B \in \mathcal{B}.$$

Figure 38 illustrates, for the special case where $B = [a, b]$. μ is called X's *distribution*. It is often easier to work with probability measures over $(\mathbb{R}, \mathcal{B})$ than with probability measures over $(\Omega, \mathcal{F})$, especially when Ω is complicated.

These definitions generalize from $\mathbb{R}$ to $\mathbb{R}^n$. The definitions are the same, except that we consider Borel sets over $\mathbb{R}^n$ rather than $\mathbb{R}$.

Given a function X from Ω to $\mathbb{R}$ and a probability measure μ over $(\mathbb{R}, \mathcal{B})$, we can use X and μ to define a probability space with Ω as the outcome space. Define $\sigma(X)$, the *σ-field generated by X*, by

$$\sigma(X) =_{df} \{X^{-1}(B) : B \in \mathcal{B}\}.$$

Define a probability measure P over $\sigma(X)$ by

$$P\left(X^{-1}(B)\right) =_{df} \mu(B), \text{for every } B \in \mathcal{B}.$$

Then $(\Omega, \sigma(X), P)$ is a probability space, and X is a random variable defined on $(\Omega, \sigma(X), P)$. This procedure generalizes from $\mathbb{R}$ to $\mathbb{R}^n$.

A4 Discrete and Nondiscrete Random Variables

A *discrete* random variable has countably many possible values. Many random variables encountered in scientific applications are *nondiscrete*, that is, they have uncountably many possible values.

Here is a fundamental constraint on random variables: at most countably values x of random variable X can receive positive probability. In other words, there are at most countably many real numbers x such that

$$P(X = x) > 0.$$

To prove this statement, let us for each natural number $n > 0$ define D_n as follows:

$$D_n =_{df} \left\{ x \in \mathbb{R} : P(X = x) > \tfrac{1}{n} \right\}.$$

Suppose for purposes of *reductio* that D_n has at least n members $x_1, x_2, \ldots, x_n$. The events $X = x_i$ and $X = x_j$ are disjoint when $i \neq j$. By finite additivity,

$$P(X = x_1 \cup X = x_2 \cup \ldots \cup X = x_n) =$$
$$P(X = x_1) + P(X = x_2) + \ldots + P(X = x_n).$$

Each individual term $P(X = x_i)$ is greater than $1/n$, so the sum on the right is greater than

$$\frac{n}{n} = 1,$$

which contradicts our axiomatic assumption that 1 is the maximal probability. By *reductio*, each set D_n contains fewer than n members. See Figure 40. Using set theory, one can then show that $\underset{n}{\cup} D_n$ is at most countably infinite. Every x such that $P(X = x) > 0$ must belong to some set D_n and hence must belong to $\underset{n}{\cup} D_n$. Therefore, there are at most countably many x such that $P(X = x) > 0$. Note that our proof uses only finite additivity, with no need for countable additivity.

Many philosophers endorse the doctrine, sometimes called *Regularity*, that agents should assign credence 0 only to impossible hypotheses (Kemeny, 1955; Skyrms, 1995; Stalnaker, 1970). The idea is that, if H is in some sense possible, then a rational agent will acknowledge its possibility by allocating it at least some nonzero credence. The foregoing proof shows that Regularity dramatically conflicts with the probability calculus axioms, no matter how exactly we gloss "possibility." The axioms demand that at most countably many values of a random variable receive nonzero probability. When a random variable is

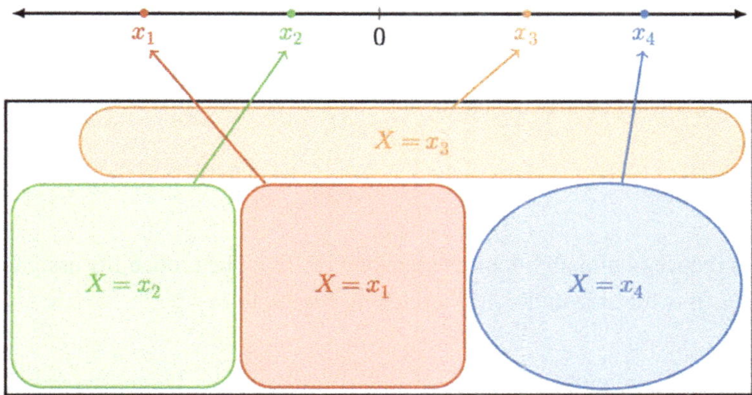

Figure 40 D_5 contains at most four members x_1, x_2, x_3, and x_4. Figure 40 depicts a case where it has exactly four members. Similarly, each set D_n contains at most $n-1$ members.

nondiscrete, uncountably many of its possible values must receive probability 0. This remains so even if one favors finite additivity over countable additivity. In response, Skyrms (1980) recommends that we preserve Regularity by revising the probability calculus axioms. The recommendation has not found much uptake within probability theory or its scientific applications, including Bayesian applications. Scientific practitioners of the Bayesian framework routinely set $P(X = x) = 0$ for uncountably many possible values x. So Regularity conflicts not just with orthodox probability theory but also with scientific practice.

These observations prompt us to reflect upon the meaning of extremal credences 0 and 1. Let X be a nondiscrete random variable, such as asteroid speed, and suppose that an agent sets $P(X = x) = 0$. The probability calculus axioms demand that the agent also set $P(X \neq x) = 1$. Certainty in the event $X \neq x$ does not entail that the agent regards value x as impossible. The agent fully realizes that the asteroid may have speed x. By assigning probability 0 to speed x, the agent does not completely reject the possibility of speed x. She merely regards this possibility as so negligible that it merits no positive credence. Assuming the agent's credences conform to the probability calculus axioms, she must similarly regard uncountably many other values of X as negligible possibilities.

A random variable is said to be *continuous* when $P(X = x) = 0$ for all x. A continuous random variable violates Regularity in a very extreme way: every event $X = x$ receives probability 0. Note that some random variables are neither discrete nor continuous (Billingsley, 1995, pp. 257–258): such a variable has uncountably many possible values x, and certain values receive positive probability.

A5 Probability Density Functions

A *probability density function* (pdf) is a nonnegative function $p(x)$ from $\mathbb{R}$ to $\mathbb{R}$ such that the area under the curve is 1:

$$\int_{-\infty}^{\infty} p(x)dx = 1.$$

A pdf induces a probability measure μ over $(\mathbb{R}, \mathcal{B})$. The probability assigned by μ to $[a, b]$ is the area under $p(x)$ stretching from a to b:

$$\mu([a, b]) = \int_{a}^{b} p(x)dx.$$

Probability assignments to the intervals $[a, b]$ determine unique probability assignments to all Borel sets. Thus, each pdf induces a unique probability measure μ.

Because probability density determines probability via integration, changes to the pdf do not affect probabilities when they do not affect integration. Compare Figure 9 with Figure 41. These are two different pdfs: they assign different densities to c. Nevertheless, they induce the same probabilities, because a change in density at a single point does not affect integration. More

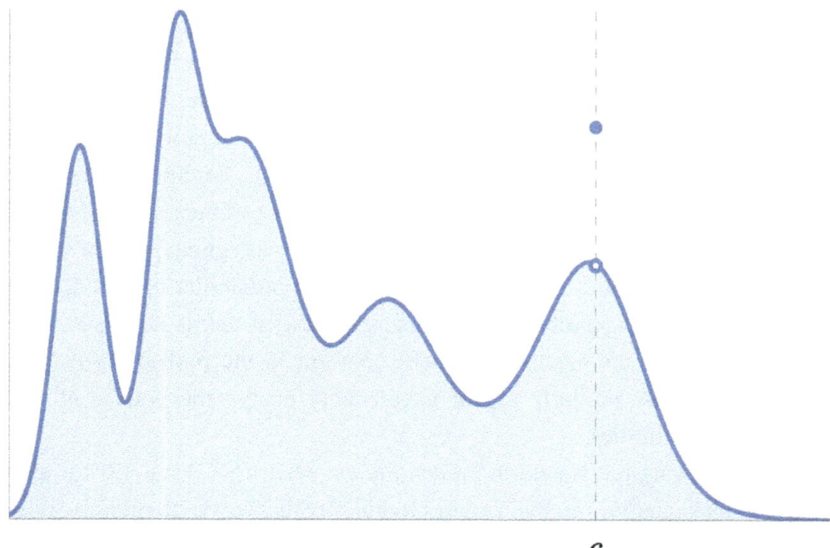

Figure 41 This pdf alters the pdf from Figure 9 at a single point c. The alteration does not affect the area under the curve, so the two pdfs determine the same probability distribution.

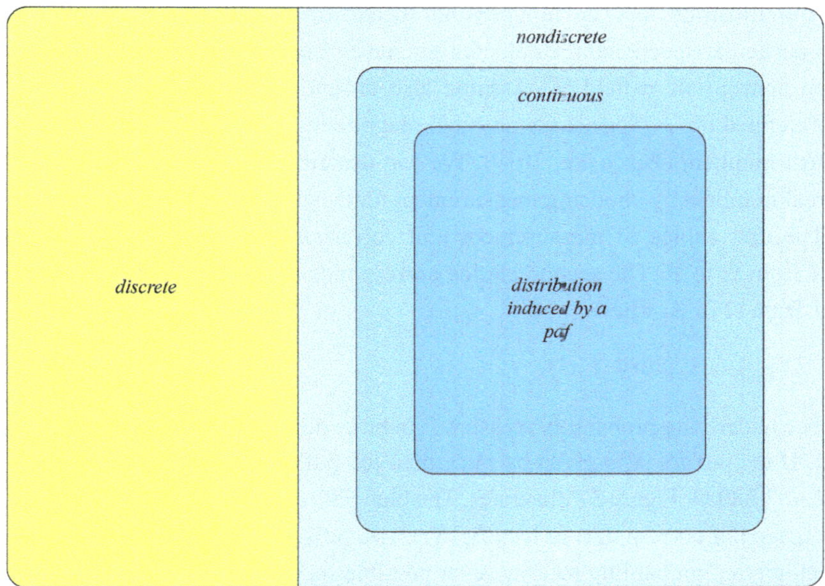

Figure 42 Typology of random variables. A random variable is either discrete or nondiscrete. A continuous random variable is nondiscrete; the converse is not true. A random variable is continuous if its distribution is induced by a pdf; the converse is not true.

generally: when pdf $p(x)$ induces probability measure μ, there are infinitely many distinct pdfs that induce the same measure μ.

Suppose random variable X is defined on probability space $(\Omega, \mathcal{F}, P)$ with distribution μ. Suppose μ is induced by a pdf $p(x)$. It is not hard to show that X is a continuous random variable: $P(X = x) = 0$ for all x (Billingsley, 1995, p. 212). Equivalently, $\mu(\{x\}) = 0$ for all x. The converse is not true: in some cases, the distribution of a continuous random variable is not induced by any pdf (Proschan & Shaw, 2016, pp. 94–95). See Figure 42.

Given a random variable X defined on probability space $(\Omega, \mathcal{F}, P)$, define a new random variable Y resulting from multiplication by a constant k:

$$Y(\omega) = kX(\omega).$$

Suppose that X's distribution has a pdf $p(x)$. One can show that Y's distribution has a pdf $q(y)$ given by

$$q(y) = \frac{p(y/k)}{k}. \tag{6}$$

See Ma, Kording & Goldreich (2023, pp. 333–336). The change in variable (from X to Y) necessitates a change in pdf.

To illustrate, let Ω contain possible speeds for an object. Each outcome ω is a particular speed that the object might have. Assume that Ω is endowed with an appropriate σ-field $\mathcal{F}$. Assume also an underlying probability measure P defined on $\mathcal{F}$. Speeds are physical magnitudes and hence are distinct from real numbers (Peacocke, 2019). We can describe physical magnitudes with real numbers by choosing measurement units, such as meters/sec or feet/sec. The first choice of measurement unit corresponds to one random variable X from Ω to $\mathbb{R}$. The second choice corresponds to a second random variable Y from Ω to $\mathbb{R}$, where

$$Y(\omega) = 3.28084\, X(\omega).$$

The underlying probability measure P induces different distributions for X and Y. If the pdf for X is given by $p(x)$, then the pdf for Y is given by (6), taking $k = 3.28084$. Figure 37 illustrates. The blue pdf corresponds to meters/sec. The orange pdf corresponds to feet/sec. The two pdfs are associated with the same underlying probability measure over possible speeds.

A6 Conditional Density and Beyond

Using conditional densities, we can extend the notion of conditional probability well beyond the elementary case where the ratio formula prevails.

Suppose we are given a two-dimensional pdf $p(x,y)$. We want to define a new pdf over *y conditional on X having value a*. So we want to define a *one-dimensional* conditional density over y, which we may notate as:

$$p(y \mid X = a).$$

Intuitively: this is a density over *y given that X has value a*. To define $p(y \mid X = a)$, we confine attention to points such that $X = a$. We consider p's values *on those points alone*:

$$p(a,y).$$

One might hope to set the conditional density $p(y \mid X = a)$ equal to $p(a,y)$, where we hold a fixed and allow y to vary. The only hitch is that $p(a,y)$, viewed as a function of y, may not be a pdf: the area under the curve may not be 1. We must settle for proportionality rather than equality:

$$p(y \mid X = a) \propto p(a,y).$$

Intuitively, $p(y \mid X = a)$ confines attention to outcomes where $X = a$ and then allocates probability density in proportion to the original density function $p(a,y)$. To obtain $p(y \mid X = a)$ from $p(a,y)$, we need merely divide $p(a,y)$ by a constant to ensure that the area under the curve is 1. This constant is called a *normalization constant.*

More formally, we may define conditional density as follows. Take $p(x,y)$ as given and define $p(x)$, the *marginal pdf for X*:

$$p(x) =_{df} \int_{-\infty}^{\infty} p(x,y)dy.$$

$p(x)$ is computed by holding x fixed and integrating $p(x,y)$ over all possible values of y. Assuming that $p(x) > 0$, we may define *the conditional density of Y given X = x* by the equation

$$p(y \mid X = x) =_{df} \frac{p(x,y)}{p(x)}. \tag{7}$$

$p(x)$ is the normalization constant: it ensures that probabilities sum to 1. When it is clear which random variable X is at issue, we may notate (7) more compactly as

$$p(y \mid x) = \frac{p(x,y)}{p(x)}. \tag{8}$$

$p(y \mid x)$ results from $p(x,y)$ by holding x fixed and then normalizing. See Figures 18, 19, 20, and 21. These definitions generalize to higher dimensions.[16]

It is often most natural to regard $p(x)$ and $p(y \mid x)$ as primitive rather than defined. For example, $p(x)$ might be a pdf for asteroid speed and $p(y \mid x)$ might be the conditional density of measuring speed y given that the asteroid has speed x. Taken together, $p(x)$ and $p(y \mid x)$ determine a joint density $p(x,y)$: we simply view equation (8) as a definition of $p(x,y)$ rather than of $p(y \mid x)$. In practice, we need not usually consider the joint density. It lies in the background of our theorizing, but we only explicitly consider $p(x)$, $p(y \mid x)$, and $p(x \mid y)$.

The ratio formula and the theory of conditional densities suffice for most applications of Bayesian decision theory. However, there are situations where we would like to define conditional probabilities yet neither the ratio formula *nor* the theory of conditional densities applies. To illustrate with a cognitive

---

[16] This paragraph glosses over some major philosophical and mathematical complications. Due to a phenomenon known as *the Borel–Kolmogorov paradox*, we cannot condition directly on $X = x$ when $P(X = x) = 0$ (Kolmogorov, 1933/1956). We instead condition on $X = x$ *considered as embedded within the σ-field* σ(X). If we were to consider $X = x$ as embedded within a different σ-field, then different conditional probabilities might result. The notation $p(y \mid X = x)$ is rather misleading because it elides this relativity to an embedding σ-field. Similarly for the notation $p(y \mid x)$. See Rescorla (2015c) for discussion of the Borel–Kolmogorov paradox and its ramifications.

science example, consider the *Bayesian causal inference model* given by Kording et al. (2007). The model evaluates whether visual input e_V and auditory input e_A derive from a single distal source. C is a binary random variable that registers the number of sources: $C = 1$ registers a single source, and $C = 2$ registers two distinct sources. Upon receiving inputs e_V and e_A, the model computes the posterior probability $P(C = 1 \mid e_V, e_A)$ that those inputs derive from a single distal source. Assume that there are uncountably many possible inputs, as Kording et al. (2007) do and as is standard in Bayesian perceptual psychology. Then we cannot define conditional probabilities $P(C = 1 \mid e_V, e_A)$ using either the ratio formula or conditional densities. The ratio formula does not apply because there is probability zero of any given input pair (e_V, e_A), except perhaps for countably many such pairs. Nor does the theory of conditional densities apply: C is discrete, so no joint density exists. As this example illustrates, a general theory of conditional probability must look beyond both the ratio formula and conditional densities.

The most successful general theory traces back to the same treatise where Kolmogorov (1933/1956) codified the probability calculus axioms. The ratio formula and the theory of conditional densities are special cases of Kolmogorov's theory (Billingsley, 1995, p. 432; Rescorla, 2015c). Kolmogorov's theory is general enough to handle the Bayesian causal inference model, along with countless other applications. Perhaps because Kolmogorov's theory is forbiddingly technical, it was long neglected by the philosophical community. Recently, it has begun to receive sympathetic attention from philosophers (Easwaran, 2011b; Huttegger, 2015; Meehan & Zhang, 2020; Nielsen, 2021; Rescorla, 2018a; Rescorla, forthcoming). Easwaran (2019) gives a detailed introduction, with comparisons to alternative theories of conditional probability.

A7 Proof of Bayes's Theorem

Suppose that $P(H) > 0$ and $P(E) > 0$. The ratio formula determines conditional probabilities $P(H \mid E)$ and $P(E \mid H)$:

$$P(H \mid E) = \frac{P(H \cap E)}{P(E)}$$

$$P(E \mid H) = \frac{P(E \cap H)}{P(H)}.$$

Algebraic manipulation yields

$$P(H \mid E)P(E) = P(H \cap E) = P(E \cap H) = P(E \mid H)P(H),$$

which immediately entails *Bayes's Theorem*:

$$P(H\,|\,E) = \frac{P(H)P(E\,|\,H)}{P(E)}. \tag{9}$$

It is remarkable that this theorem follows almost trivially from the ratio formula yet offers such profound insight into rational inference.

Now consider the case where we have a two-dimensional pdf $p(x,y)$. Define conditional densities and marginals as in Section A6:

$$p(x)=_{df} \int_{-\infty}^{\infty} p(x,y)dy$$

$$p(y)=_{df} \int_{-\infty}^{\infty} p(x,y)dx$$

$$p(y\,|\,x)=_{df} \frac{p(x,y)}{p(x)}$$

$$p(x\,|\,y)=_{df} \frac{p(x,y)}{p(y)},$$

where the third definition presupposes $p(x) > 0$ and the fourth presupposes $p(y) > 0$. From these latter two definitions,

$$p(x\,|\,y)p(y) = p(x,y) = p(y\,|\,x)p(x).$$

By algebra,

$$p(x\,|\,y) = \frac{p(y\,|\,x)p(x)}{p(y)}, \tag{10}$$

which is Bayes's theorem for pdfs. Note that $1/p(y)$ does not depend upon x. It figures solely as a normalization constant. Although (9) and (10) look similar and have similar proofs, they are distinct: (9) concerns conditional probabilities, while (10) concerns conditional densities.

Bayes's theorem generalizes beyond the formulations given here, using Kolmogorov's theory of conditional probability (Ghosal & van der Vaart, 2017, p. 7). There are also some situations where no analogue to Bayes's theorem is available (Ghosal & van der Vaart, 2017, pp. 7–8). In those situations, one can still conform to Conditionalization: one can respond to new evidence by replacing the prior with the posterior. Unfortunately, one can no longer use anything like (9) or (10) to compute the posterior.

References

Abend, O., Kwiatkowski, T., Smith, N., Goldwater, S. & Steedman, S. (2017). Bootstrapping language acquisition. *Cognition*, **164**, 116–143.

Ackerman, N., Freer, C. & Roy, D. (2019). On the computability of conditional probability. *Journal of the ACM*, **66**, 1–40.

Adams, W., Graf, E. & Ernst, M. (2004). Experience can change the "light-from-above" prior. *Nature Neuroscience*, **7**, 1057–1058.

Aitchison, L. & Lengyel, M. (2017). With or without you: predictive coding and Bayesian inference in the brain. *Current Opinion in Neurobiology*, **46**, 219–227.

Ashby, D. (2006). Bayesian statistics in medicine: a 25 year review. *Statistics in Medicine*, **25**, 3589–3631.

Baker, C. & Tenenbaum, J. (2014). Modeling human plan recognition using Bayesian theory of mind. In G. Sukthankar, R. P. Goldman, C. Geib, D. Pynadath & H. Bui, eds., *Plan, Activity, and Intent Recognition: Theory and Practice*. Waltham: Morgan Kaufmann, pp. 177–204.

Battaglia, P. W., Hamrick, J. & Tenenbaum, J. (2013). Simulation as an engine of physical scene understanding. *Proceedings of the National Academy of Sciences*, **110**, 18327–18332.

Bayes, T. (1763). An essay towards solving a problem in the doctrine of chances. *Philosophical Transactions of the Royal Society of London*, **53**, 470–418.

Beck, J., Ma, W. J., Latham, P. E. & Pouget, A. (2007). Probabilistic population codes and the exponential family of distributions. In P. Cisek, T. Drew & J. F. Kalaska, eds., *Computational Neuroscience: Theoretical Insights into Brain Function*. New York: Elsevier.

Berger, J. (1985). *Statistical Decision Theory: Foundations, Concepts, and Methods*, 2nd ed., New York: Springer.

Berniker, M., & Voss, M. (2010). Learning priors for Bayesian computations in the nervous system. *PLOS One*, **10**, e12686.

Bernstein, N. (1967). *The Coordination and Regulation of Movements*. Oxford: Pergamon.

Billingsley, P. (1995). *Probability and Measure*. 3rd ed. New York: Wiley.

Block, N. (2018). If perception is probabilistic, why does it not seem probabilistic? *Philosophical Transactions of the Royal Society B*, **373**, 20170341.

Block, N. (2023). *The Border Between Perception and Cognition*. Cambridge, MA: MIT Press.

Bowers, J. & Davis, C. (2012). Bayesian just-so stories in psychology and neuroscience. *Psychological Bulletin*, **138**, 389–414.

Brooks, S., Gelman, A., Jones, G. & Meng, X.-L., eds. (2011). *Handbook of Markov Chain Monte Carlo*. New York: CRC Press.

Burge, T. (2010). *Origins of Objectivity*. Oxford: Oxford University Press.

Burge, T. (2022). *Perception: First Form of Mind*. Oxford: Oxford University Press.

Burns, J. & Blohm, G. (2010). Multi-sensory weights depend on contextual noise in reference frame transformations. *Frontiers in Human Neuroscience*, **4**, 1–16.

Cao, R. (2020). New labels for old ideas: predictive processing and the interpretation of neural signals. *Review of Philosophy and Psychology*, **11**, 517–546.

Carey, S. (2009). *The Origin of Concepts*. Oxford: Oxford University Press.

Chalmers, D. (2011). Frege's puzzle and the objects of credence. *Mind*, **120**, 587–635.

Chater, N. & Oaksford, M. eds. (2008). *The Probabilistic Mind*. Oxford: Oxford University Press.

Chater, N., Zhu, J.-Q., Spicer, J., Sundh, J., León-Villagrá, P. & Sanborn, A. (2020). Probabilistic biases meet the Bayesian brain. *Current Directions in Psychological Science*, **29**, 506–512.

Chemero, A. (2009). *Radical Embodied Cognitive Science*. Cambridge, MA: MIT Press.

Chen, X., McNamara, T., Kelly, J. & Wolbers, T. (2017). Cue combination in human spatial navigation. *Cognitive Psychology*, **95**, 105–144.

Cheyette, S. & Piantadosi, S. (2017). Knowledge transfer in a probabilistic language of thought. *Proceedings of the Annual Meeting of the Cognitive Science Society*, **39**, 222–227.

Churchland, P. (1981). Eliminative materialism and the propositional attitudes. *Journal of Philosophy*, **78**, 67–90.

Clark, A. (2015). *Surfing Uncertainty*. Oxford: Oxford University Press.

Colombo, M. & Seriès, P. (2012). Bayes in the brain—on Bayesian modeling in neuroscience. *The British Journal for the Philosophy of Science*, **63**, 697–723.

Dasgupta, I., Schulz, E. & Gershman, S. (2017). Where do hypotheses come from? *Cognitive Psychology*, **96**, 1–25.

de Finetti, B. (1937/1980). Foresight. Its logical laws, its subjective sources. Rpt. in H. E. Kyburg, Jr. & H. E. Smokler, eds., *Studies in Subjective Probability*. Huntington, NY: Robert E. Krieger, pp. 53–118.

de Finetti, B. (1972). *Probability, Induction, and Statistics*. New York: Wiley.

DeGroot, M. (1970). *Optimal Statistical Decisions*. New York: McGraw-Hill.

Dener, E., Kacelnik, A. & Shemesh, H. (2016). Pea plants show risk sensitivity. *Current Biology*, **26**, 1763–1767.

Dennett, D. (1987). *The Intentional Stance*. Cambridge, MA: MIT Press.

Duffy, S., Huttenlocher, J., Hedges, L. & Crawford, L. E. (2010). Category effects on stimulus estimation: shifting and skewed frequency distributions. *Psychonomic Bulletin and Review*, **17**, 224–230.

Earman, J. (1992). *Bayes or Bust?* Cambridge, MA: MIT Press.

Easwaran, K. (2011a). Bayesianism I: introduction and arguments in favor. *Philosophy Compass*, **6**, 312–320.

Easwaran, K. (2011b). The varieties of conditional probability. In P. Bandyopadhyay & M. Forster, eds., *Philosophy of Statistics*. Amsterdam: Elsevier, pp. 137–148.

Easwaran, K. (2013). Why countable additivity? *Thought*, **2**, 53–61.

Easwaran, K. (2019). Conditional probabilities. In R. Pettigrew & J. Weisberg, eds., *The Open Handbook of Formal Epistemology*. London, ON: The PhilPapers Foundation, pp. 131–198.

Eberhardt, F. & Danks, D. (2011). Confirmation in the cognitive sciences: the problematic case of Bayesian models. *Minds and Machines*, **21**, 389–410.

Egan, F. (2010). Computational models: a modest role for content. *Studies in History and Philosophy of Science*, **41**, 253–259.

Egan, F. (2020). A deflationary account of mental representation. In J. Smorthchkova, T. Schlicht & K. Dolega, eds., *What Are Mental Representations?* Oxford: Oxford University Press, pp. 26–53.

Erikkson, L. & Hájek, A. (2007). What are degrees of belief? *Studia Logica*, **86**, 183–213.

Ernst, M. (2006). A Bayesian view on multimodal cue integration. In G. Knoblich, I. Thornton, M. Grosjean & M. Shiffrar, eds., *Human Body Perception From the Inside Out*. Oxford: Oxford University Press, pp. 105–132.

Ernst, M. (2007). Learning to integrate arbitrary signals from vision and touch. *Journal of Vision*, **7**, 1–14.

Ernst, M. & Banks, M. (2002). Humans integrate visual and haptic information in a statistically optimal fashion. *Nature*, **415**, 429–433.

Fernandes, H., Stevenson, I., Vilares, I. & Kording, K. (2014). The generalization of prior uncertainty during reaching. *The Journal of Neuroscience*, **34**, 11470–11484.

Fiehler, K., Wolf, C., Klinghammer, M. & Blohm, G. (2014). Integration of egocentric and allocentric information during memory-guided reaching to images of a natural environment. *Frontiers in Human Neuroscience*, **8**, 1–12.

Field, H. (2001). *Truth and the Absence of Fact*. Oxford: Clarendon Press.

Fiser, J., Berkes, P., Orbán, G. & Lengyel, M. (2010). Statistically optimal perception and learning: from behavior to neural representations. *Trends in Cognitive Sciences*, **14**, 119–130.

Fodor, J. (1975). *The Language of Thought*. New York: Thomas Y. Crowell.

Fodor, J. (1987). *Psychosemantics*. Cambridge, MA: MIT Press.

Fodor, J. (2008). *LOT2*. Oxford: Clarendon Press.

Fodor, J. & Pylyshyn, Z. (1981). How direct is visual perception? Some reflections on Gibson's "ecological approach." *Cognition*, **9**, 139–196.

Frege, G. (1892/1997). On *Sinn* and *Bedeutung*. Rpt. in M. Beaney, ed., *The Frege Reader*, trans. M. Black. Malden, MA: Blackwell.

Fristedt, B. & Gray, L. (1997). *A Modern Approach to Probability Theory*. Boston: Birkhäuser.

Friston, K. (2010). The free-energy principle: a unified brain theory? *Nature Reviews Neuroscience*, **11**, 127–138.

Gaifman, H. & Snir, M. (1982). Probabilities over rich languages, testing, and randomness. *The Journal of Symbolic Logic*, **47**, 495–548.

Gallistel, C. R. (1990). *The Organization of Learning*. Cambridge, MA: MIT Press.

Gallistel, C. R. (2008). Dead reckoning, cognitive maps, animal navigation, and the representation of space: an introduction. In M. Jeffries & W.-K. Yeap, eds., *Robotics and Cognitive Approaches to Spatial Mapping*. Berlin: Springer, pp. 137–143.

Gallistel, C. R. & King, A. (2009). *Memory and the Computational Brain*. Malden, MA: Wiley-Blackwell.

Ganguli, D. & Simoncelli, E. (2014). Efficient sensory encoding and Bayesian inference with heterogeneous neural populations. *Neural Computation*, **26**, 2103–2134.

Gardner, J. (2019). Optimality and heuristics in perceptual neuroscience. *Nature Neuroscience*, **22**, 514–523.

Gelman, A., Carlin, J., Stern, H., Dunson, D., Vehatri, A. & Rubin, D. (2014). *Bayesian Data Analysis*, 3rd ed. New York: CRC Press.

Ghosal, S. & van der Vaart, A. (2017). *Fundamentals of Nonparametric Bayesian Inference*. Cambridge: Cambridge University Press.

Gibson, J. J. (1979). *The Ecological Approach to Visual Perception*. Boston: Houghton Mifflin.

Glasauer, S. (2019). Sequential Bayesian updating as a model for human perception. *Progress in Brain Research*, **249**, 3–18.

Glasauer, S. & Shi, Z. (2022). Individual beliefs about temporal continuity explain variation of perceptual biases. *Scientific Reports*, **12**, 10746.

Goodman, N., Tenenbaum, J., Feldman, J. & Griffiths, T. (2008). A rational analysis of rule-based concept learning. *Cognitive Science*, **32**, 108–154.

Goodman, N., Ullman, T. & Tenenbaum, J. (2011). Learning a theory of causality. *Psychological Review*, **118**, 110–199.

Greaves, H. & Wallace, D. (2006). Justifying conditionalization: conditionalization maximizes expected epistemic utility. *Mind*, **115**, 607–632.

Griffiths, T., Kemp, C. and Tenenbaum, J. (2008). Bayesian models of cognition. In R. Sun, ed., *The Cambridge Handbook of Computational Psychology*. Cambridge: Cambridge University Press, pp. 59–100.

Griffiths, T. & Tenenbaum, J. (2009). Theory-based causal induction. *Psychological Review*, **116**, 661–716.

Hacking, I. (2001). *An Introduction to Probability and Inductive Logic*. Cambridge: Cambridge University Press.

Haith, A. & Krakauer, J. (2013). Theoretical models of motor control and motor learning. In M. Richardson, M. Riley, and K. Shockley, eds., *Progress in Motor Control VII: Neural Computational and Dynamic Approaches*. New York: Springer, pp. 7–28.

Helbig, H. & Ernst, M. (2008). Haptic perception in interaction with other senses. In M. Grunwald, ed., *Human Haptic Perception: Basics and Applications*. Boston: Birkhäuser Verlag, pp. 235–249.

Helmholtz, H. von. (1867/1925). *Treatise on Physiological Optics*, trans. and ed. J. Southall. Manasha, WI: George Banta Publishing Company.

Hemmer, P. & Steyvers, M. (2009). A Bayesian account of reconstructive memory. *Topics in Cognitive Science*, **1**, 189–202.

Hillis, J., Ernst, M., Banks, M. & Landy, M. (2002). Combining sensory information: mandatory fusion within, but not between, senses. *Science*, **298**, 1627–1630.

Hohwy, J. (2014). *The Predictive Mind*. Oxford: Oxford University Press.

Hollingworth, H. (1910). The central tendency of judgment. *The Journal of Philosophy, Psychology, and Scientific Methods*, **7**, 461–469.

Huttegger, S. (2015). Merging of opinions and probability kinematics. *The Review of Symbolic Logic*, **8**, 611–648.

Hutto, D. & Myin, E. (2017). *Evolving Enactivism: Basic Minds Meet Content*. Cambridge, MA: MIT Press.

Icard, T. (2016). Subjective probability as sampling propensity. *The Review of Philosophy and Psychology*, **7**, 863–903.

Jazayeri, M. & Shadlen, M. (2010). Temporal context calibrates interval timing. *Nature Neuroscience*, **13**, 1020–1026.

Jetzschke, S., Ernst, M., Froehlich, J. & Boeddeker, N. (2014). Finding home: landmark ambiguity in human navigation. *Frontiers in Behavioral Neuroscience*, **11**, 1–15.

Jones, M. & Love, B. (2011). Bayesian fundamentalism or enlightenment? On the explanatory status and theoretical contribution of Bayesian models of cognition. *Behavioral and Brain Sciences*, **34**, 159–188.

Kahneman, D. & Tversky, A. (1979). Prospect theory: an analysis of decision under risk. *Econometrica*, **47**, 263–291.

Katz, Y., Goodman, N., Kersting, K., Kemp, C. & Tenenbaum, J. (2008). Modeling semantic cognition as logical dimensionality reduction. *Proceedings of the Annual Meeting of the Cognitive Science Society*, **30**. https://escholarship.org/uc/item/50r1c7qh.

Kemeny, J. (1955). Fair bets and inductive probabilities. *The Journal of Symbolic Logic*, **20**, 263–273.

Kessler, F., Frankenstein, J. & Rothkopf, C. (2024). Human navigation strategies and their errors result from dynamic interactions of spatial uncertainties. *Nature Communications*, **15**, 5677.

Knill, D. & Richards, W., eds. (1996). *Perception as Bayesian inference*. Cambridge: Cambridge University Press.

Kolmogorov, A. N. (1933/1956). *Foundations of the Theory of Probability*. 2nd English ed, trans. N. Morrison. New York: Chelsea.

Kording, K., Beierholm, U., Ma, W. J., Quartz, S., Tenenbaum J. & Shams L. (2007). Causal inference in multisensory perception. *PLoS One*, **2**, e943.

Kording, K. & Wolpert, D. (2004). Bayesian integration in sensorimotor learning. *Nature*, **427**, 244–247.

Kwisthout, J., Wareham, T. & van Rooij, I. (2011). Bayesian intractability is not an ailment that approximation can cure. *Cognitive Science*, **35**, 779–784.

Kwon, O.-S. & Knill, D. (2013). The brain uses adaptive internal models of scene statistics for sensorimotor estimation and planning. *Proceedings of the National Academy of Sciences*, **110**, E1064–E1073.

Kwon, O.-S., Tadin, D. & Knill, D. (2015). Unifying account of visual motion and position perception. *Proceedings of the National Academy of Sciences*, **112**, 8142–8147.

Lakshminarasimhan, K., Petsalis, M., Park, H., DeAngelis, G., Pitkow, X. & Angelaki, D. (2018). A dynamic Bayesian observer model reveals origins of bias in visual path integration. *Neuron*, **99**, 194–206.

Laplace, P.-S. (1814/1902). *A Philosophical Essay on Probabilities*, trans. F. Truscott & F. Emory. New York: Wiley.

Lappe, M., Stiels, M., Frenz, H. & Loomis, J. (2011). Keeping track of the distance from home by leaking integration along veering paths. *Experimental Brain Research*, **212**, 81–89.

Lee, T. S. & Mumford, D. (2003). Hierarchical Bayesian inference in the visual cortex. *Journal of the Optical Society of America*, **20**, 1434–1448.

Lewis, D. (1999). Why conditionalize? In *Papers in Metaphysics and Epistemology*. Cambridge: Cambridge University Press, pp. 403–407.

Lieder, F., Griffiths, T., Huys, Q. & Goodman, N. (2018). The anchoring bias reflects rational use of cognitive resources. *Psychonomic Bulletin and Review*, **25**, 322–349.

Liu, Y. (2020). Countable additivity, idealization, and conceptual realism. *Economics and Philosophy*, **36**, 127–147.

McGrayne, S. (2011). *The Theory that Would Not Die*. New Haven, CT: Yale University Press.

McNamee, D. & Wolpert, D. (2019). Internal models in biological control. *Annual Review of Control, Robotics, and Autonomous Systems*, **2**, 339–364.

Ma, W. J. (2019). Bayesian decision models: a primer. *Neuron*, **104**, 164–175.

Ma, W. J., Beck, J., Latham, P. & Pouget, A. (2006). Bayesian inference with probabilistic population codes. *Nature Neuroscience*, **9**, 1432–1438.

Ma, W. J., Kording, K. & Goldreich, D. (2023). *Bayesian Models of Perception and Action: An Introduction*. Cambridge, MA: MIT Press.

Mahtani, A. (2024). *The Objects of Credence*. Oxford: Oxford University Press.

Makin, J., Fellows, M. & Sabes, P. (2013). Learning multisensory integration and coordinate transformation via density estimation. *PLOS Computational Biology*, **9**, e1003035.

Mamassian, P., Landy, M. & Maloney, L. (2002). Bayesian modeling of visual perception. In R. Rao, B. Olshausen & M. Lewicki, eds., *Probabilistic Models of the Brain*. Cambridge, MA: MIT Press, pp. 13–36.

Mandelbaum, E. (2019). Troubles with Bayesianism: an introduction to the psychological immune system. *Mind and Language* **34**: 141–157.

Mandelbaum, E., Won, I., Gross, S. & Firestone, C. (2020). Can resources save rationality? "Anti-Bayesian" updating in cognition and perception. *Behavioral and Brain Sciences*, **43**, 31–32.

Meehan, A. & Zhang, S. (2020). Jeffrey meets Kolmogorov: a general theory of conditioning. *Journal of Philosophical Logic*, **49**, 941–979.

Morales, J., Solovey, G., Maniscalco, B., Rahnev, D., de Lange, F. & Lau, H. (2015). Low attention impairs optimal incorporation of prior knowledge in perceptual decisions. *Attention, Perception, and Psychophysics*, **77**, 2021–2036.

Murphy, K. (2023). *Probabilistic machine learning: advanced topics*. Cambridge, MA: MIT Press.

Narayanan, S. & Jurafsky, D. (1998). Bayesian models of human sentence processing. In *Proceedings of the Annual Meeting of the Cognitive Science Society*, **20**, 752–757.

Nashed, J., Crevecoeur, F. & Scott, S. (2012). Influence of the behavioral goal and environmental obstacles on rapid feedback responses. *Journal of Neurophysiology*, **108**, 999–1009.

Nielsen, M. (2021). A new argument for Kolmogorov Conditionalization. *The Review of Symbolic Logic*, **14**, 930–945.

Norris, D. (2006). The Bayesian reader: explaining word recognition as an optimal Bayesian decision process. *Psychological Review*, **113**, 327–357.

Oaksford, M. & Chater, N. (2007). *Bayesian Rationality: The Probabilistic Approach to Human Reasoning*. Oxford: Oxford University Press.

Oaksford, M. & Chater, N. (2020). New paradigms in the psychology of reasoning. *Annual Review of Psychology*, **71**, 305–330.

Olkkonen, M., McCarthy, P. & Allred, S. (2014). The central tendency bias in color perception: effects of internal and external noise. *Journal of Vision*, **14**, 1–15.

Orbán, G., Berkes, P., Fiser, J. & Lengyel, M. (2016). Neural variability and sampling-based probabilistic representations in the visual cortex. *Neuron*, **92**, 530–542.

Orlandi, N. (2014). *The Innocent Eye: Why Vision is not Cognitive Process*. Oxford: Oxford University Press.

Peacocke, C. (1994). Content, computation, and externalism. *Mind and Language*, **9**, 303–335.

Peacocke, C. (1999). Computation as involving content: a response to Egan. *Mind and Language*, **14**, 195–202.

Peacocke, C. (2019). *The Primacy of Metaphysics*. Oxford: Oxford University Press.

Peters, M., Ma, W. J. & Shams, L. (2016). The size-weight illusion is not anti-Bayesian after all. *PeerJ*, **4**, e2124.

Pettigrew, R. (2019). Epistemic utility arguments for probabilism. In E. Zalta, ed., *The Stanford Encyclopedia of Philosophy* (Winter 2019). https://plato .stanford.edu/archives/win2019/entries/epistemic-utility.

Pettigrew, R. (2020). *Dutch Book Arguments*. Cambridge: Cambridge University Press.

Petzschner, F. & Glasauer, S. (2011). Iterative Bayesian estimation as an explanation for range and regression effects: a study on human path integration. *The Journal of Neuroscience*, **31**, 17220–17229.

Petzschner, F., Glasauer, S. & Stephan, K. (2015). A Bayesian perspective on magnitude estimation. *Trends in Cognitive Sciences*, **19**, 285–293.

Piantadosi, S. & Jacobs, R. (2016). Four problems solved by the probabilistic language of thought. *Current Directions in Psychological Science*, **25**, 54–59.

Pouget, A., Beck, J., Ma., W. J. & Latham, P. (2013). Probabilistic brains: knowns and unknowns. *Nature Neuroscience*, **16**, 1170–1178.

Proschan, M. & Shaw, P. (2016). *Essentials of Probability Theory for Statisticians*. New York: CRC Press.

Putnam, H. (1975). *Mathematics, Matter, and Method: Philosophical Papers, vol. 1*. Cambridge: Cambridge University Press.

Pylyshyn, Z. (1984). *Computation and Cognition*. Cambridge, MA: MIT Press.

Quine, W. V. (1960). *Word and Object*. Cambridge, MA: MIT Press.

Rahnev, D. & Denisov, R. (2018). Suboptimality in perceptual decision making. *Behavioral and Brain Sciences*, **41**, e223.

Ramsey, F. P. (1931). Truth and probability. In R. Braithwaite, ed., *The Foundations of Mathematics and Other Logical Essays*. London: Kegan, Paul, Trench, Trubner & Co., pp.156–198.

Ramsey, W. (2007). *Representation Reconsidered*. Cambridge: Cambridge University Press.

Rao, R. and Ballard, D. (1999). Predictive coding in the visual cortex: a functional interpretation of some extra-classical receptive-field effects. *Nature Neuroscience*, **2**, 79–87.

Rescorla, M. (2009). Cognitive maps and the language of thought. *The British Journal for the Philosophy of Science*, **60**, 377–407.

Rescorla, M. (2015a). Bayesian perceptual psychology. In M. Matthen, ed., *The Oxford Handbook of the Philosophy of Perception*. Oxford: Oxford University Press, pp. 694–716.

Rescorla, M. (2015b). Review of Nico Orlandi's *The Innocent Eye: Why Vision is not a Cognitive Process*. *Notre Dame Philosophical Reviews*, January 2015.

Rescorla, M. (2015c). Some epistemological ramifications of the Borel–Kolmogorov paradox. *Synthese*, **192**, 735–767.

Rescorla, M. (2016). Bayesian sensorimotor psychology. *Mind and Language*, **31**, 3–36.

Rescorla, M. (2017). Review of Andy Clark's *Surfing Uncertainty*. *Notre Dame Philosophical Reviews*, January 2017.

Rescorla, M. (2018a). A Dutch book theorem and converse Dutch book theorem for Kolmogorov Conditionalization. *The Review of Symbolic Logic*, **11**, 705–735.

Rescorla, M. (2018b). An interventionist approach to psychological explanation. *Synthese*, **195**, 1909–1940.

Rescorla, M. (2019). Motor computation. In M. Colombo & M. Sprevak, eds., *The Routledge Handbook of the Computational Mind*. New York: Routledge, pp. 424–435.

Rescorla, M. (2020a). The computational theory of mind. In E. Zalta, ed. *The Stanford Encyclopedia of Philosophy*. https://plato.stanford.edu/entries/computational-mind.

Rescorla, M. (2020b). Perceptual co-reference. *The Review of Philosophy and Psychology*, **11**, 569–589.

Rescorla, M. (2020c). A realist perspective on Bayesian cognitive science. In A. Nes & T. Chan, eds., *Inference and Consciousness*. New York: Routledge, pp. 40–73.

Rescorla, M. (2020d). Reifying representations. In J. Smorthchkova, T. Schlicht & K. Dolega, eds., *What Are Mental Representations?* Oxford: Oxford University Press, pp. 135–177.

Rescorla, M. (2021a). Bayesian modeling of the mind: from norm to neurons. *WIREs Cognitive Science*, **12**, e1540.

Rescorla, M. (2021b). On the proper formulation of Conditionalization. *Synthese*, **198**, 1935–1965.

Rescorla, M. (2022). An improved Dutch book theorem for Conditionalization. *Erkenntnis*, **87**, 1013–1041.

Rescorla, M. (2024). Neural implementation of (approximate) Bayesian inference. In T. Cheng, R. Sato & J. Hohwy, eds., *Expected Experiences: The Predictive Mind in an Uncertain World*. Routledge, pp. 197–239.

Rescorla, M. (Forthcoming). Non-factive Kolmogorov conditionalization. *The Review of Symbolic Logic*. https://doi.org/10.1017/S1755020323000345.

Rittenhouse, D. (1786). Explanation of an optical deception. *Transactions of the American Philosophical Society*, **2**, 37–42.

Sanborn, A., Griffiths, T. & Navarro, D. (2010). Rational approximations to rational models: alternative algorithms for category learning. *Psychological Review*, **117**, 1144–1167.

Sanborn, A., Masinghka, J. & Griffiths, T. (2013). Reconciling intuitive physics and Newtonian mechanics for colliding objects. *Psychological Review*, **120**, 411–437.

Sato, Y. & Kording, K. (2014). How much to trust the senses: likelihood learning. *Journal of Vision*, **14**, 1–13.

Sato, Y., Toyoizumi, T. & Aihara, K. (2007). Bayesian inference explains perception of unity and ventriloquism aftereffect: identification of common sources of audiovisual stimuli. *Neural Computation*, **19**, 3335–3355.

Saunders, J. & Knill, D. (2004). Visual feedback control of hand movements. *The Journal of Neuroscience*, **24**, 3223–3234.

Savage, L. (1972). *The Foundations of Statistics*, 2nd ed. New York: Dover.

Savelli, F. & Knierim, J. (2019). Origin and role of path integration in the cognitive representations of the hippocampus: computational insights into open questions. *Journal of Experimental Biology*, **222**, 1–13.

Scott, S. (2012). The computational and neural basis of voluntary motor control and planning. *Trends in Cognitive Sciences*, **16**, 541–549.

Seydell, A., Knill, D. & Trommershäuser, J. (2010). Adapting internal statistical models for interpreting visual cues to depth. *Journal of Vision*, **10**, 1–27.

Shadmehr, R. & Mussa-Ivaldi, S. (2012). *Biological Learning and Control*. Cambridge, MA: MIT Press.

Shea, N. (2018). *Representation in Cognitive Science*. Oxford: Oxford University Press.

Shikauchi, Y., Miyakoshi, M., Makeig, S. & Iversen, J. (2021). Bayesian models of human navigation behavior in an augmented reality audiomaze. *European Journal of Neuroscience*, **54**, 8308–8317.

Skyrms, B. (1980). *Causal Necessity*. New Haven, CT: Yale University Press.

Skyrms, B. (1987). Dynamic coherence and probability kinematics. *Philosophy of Science*, **54**, 1–20.

Skyrms, B. (1995). Strict coherence, sigma coherence, and the metaphysics of quantity. *Philosophical Studies*, **77**, 39–55.

Sotiropoulos, G., Seitz, A. & Seriès, P. (2011). Changing expectations about speed alters perceived motion direction. *Current Biology*, **21**, R883–R884.

Stalnaker, R. (1970). Probabilities and conditionals. *Philosophy of Science*, **37**, 64–80.

Stalnaker, R. (1984). *Inquiry*. Cambridge, MA: MIT Press.

Steele, K. & Stefánsson, H. (2016). Decision theory. In E. Zalta, ed., *The Stanford Encyclopedia of Philosophy* (Winter 2016). https://plato.stan ford.edu/archives/win2016/entries/decision-theory.

Stich, S. (1983). *From Folk Psychology to Cognitive Science*. Cambridge, MA: MIT Press.

Stocker, A. (2018). Credo for optimality. *Behavioral and Brain Sciences*, **41**, e244.

Stocker, A. & Simoncelli, E. (2006). Noise characteristics and prior expectations in human visual speed perception. *Nature Neuroscience*, **4**, 578–585.

Stone, J. (2011). Footprints sticking out of the sand, part 2: Children's Bayesian priors for shape and lighting direction. *Perception*, **40**, 175–190.

Stone, J. (2013). *Bayes's Rule: A Tutorial Introduction to Bayesian Analysis*. Sebtel Press.

Temperley, D. (2007). *Music and Probability*. Cambridge, MA: MIT Press.

Thrun, S., Burgard, W. & Fox, D. (2005). *Probabilistic Robotics*. Cambridge, MA: MIT Press.

Todorov, E. & Jordan, M. (2002). Optimal feedback control as a theory of motor coordination. *Nature Neuroscience*, **5**, 1226–1235.

Todorov, E. (2004). Optimality principles in sensorimotor control. *Nature Neuroscience*, **7**, 907–915.

Trommershäuser, J., Kording, K. & Landy, M, eds. (2011). *Sensory Cue Combination*. Oxford: Oxford University Press.

Trotta, R. (2008). Bayes in the sky: Bayesian inference and model selection in cosmology. *Contemporary Physics*, **49**, 71–104.

Tversky, A., and Kahneman, D. (1974). Judgment under uncertainty: heuristics and biases. *Science*, **185**, 1124–1131.

Tversky, A., and Kahneman, D. (1983). Extension versus intuitive reasoning: the conjunction fallacy in probability judgment. *Psychological Review*, **90**, 293–315.

van Fraassen, B. (1980). *The Scientific Image*. Oxford: Oxford University Press.

van Gelder, T. (1992). What might cognition be, if not computation? *Journal of Philosophy*, **92**, 345–381.

van Rooij, I., Blokpoel, M., Kwisthout, J. & Wareham, T. (2019). *Cognition and Intractability*. Cambridge: Cambridge University Press.

Vilares, I. & Kording, K. (2011). Bayesian models: the structure of the world, uncertainty, behavior, and the brain. *Annals of the New York Academy of Sciences*, **1224**, 22–39.

Weisberg, J. (2009). Varieties of Bayesianism. In D. Gabbay, S. Hartman & J. Woods, eds., *Handbook of the History of Logic*, vol. 10. New York: Elsevier, pp. 477–551.

Weiss, Y., Simoncelli, E. & Adelson, E. (2002). Motion illusions as optimal percepts. *Nature Neuroscience*, **5**, 598–604.

Weisswange, T., Rothkopf, C., Rodemann, T. & Triesch, J. (2011). Bayesian cue integration as a developmental outcome of reward mediated learning. *PLOS One*, **6**, e21575.

Wolpert, D. & Flanagan, J. R. (2009). Forward models. In T. Bayne, A. Cleeremans & P. Wilken, eds., *The Oxford Companion to Consciousness*. Oxford: Oxford University Press, pp. 294–296.

Acknowledgments

I presented portions of this material at the 2019 Norwegian Summer Institute on Language and Mind; a fall 2020 graduate seminar at UCLA; three sessions of a spring 2022 graduate seminar led by Roberto Casati at the Institut Jean Nicod; a spring 2024 Princeton University cognitive science colloquium; and a spring 2024 workshop on bounded rationality at the University of California, Berkeley. I am grateful to all participants in these events, especially Tyler Brooke-Wilson, Roberto Casati, Kenny Easwaran, Adam Elga, Verónica Gómez Sánchez, Steven Gross, Elizabeth Harman, Geoffrey Lee, Sarah-Jane Leslie, John MacFarlane, Alonso Molina, Nico Orlandi, Jiarui Qu, Georges Rey, Paul Talma, David Thorstad, Alejandro Vesga, Francesca Zaffora Blando, and Snow Zhang for their helpful feedback. I also thank Cosmo Grant, Thomas Icard, Keith Frankish, and two anonymous referees for their comments on an earlier draft of the manuscript. Finally, I thank Olivia Bollinger, who prepared Figures 31 and 42, and Jiarui Qu, who prepared all the other original figures.

Cambridge Elements ≡

Philosophy of Mind

Keith Frankish
The University of Sheffield

Keith Frankish is a philosopher specializing in philosophy of mind, philosophy of psychology, and philosophy of cognitive science. He is the author of *Mind and Supermind* (Cambridge University Press, 2004) and *Consciousness* (2005), and has also edited or coedited several collections of essays, including *The Cambridge Handbook of Cognitive Science* (Cambridge University Press, 2012), *The Cambridge Handbook of Artificial Intelligence* (Cambridge University Press, 2014) (both with William Ramsey), and *Illusionism as a Theory of Consciousness* (2017).

About the Series

This series provides concise, authoritative introductions to contemporary work in philosophy of mind, written by leading researchers and including both established and emerging topics. It provides an entry point to the primary literature and will be the standard resource for researchers, students, and anyone wanting a firm grounding in this fascinating field.